JUN 1 2 2018

P9-BYU-601

THE GIRL GUIDE

Marawa Ibrahim

Illustrated by Sinem Erkas

HARPER
An Imprint of HarperCollins Publishers

Simsbury Public Library
Children's Room
725 Hopmeadow Street
Simsbury, Ct. 06070

646.70846
1BR

50
ways
to learn to
love your
changing
body

How to read this book:
dip in, dip out, start at the back,
skip to the front, or read it
straight through—and
turn to it in times
of need!

Hello! I hope this book finds you well, snuggled up in a comfy spot with a hot chocolate or on a bus heading home . . . however you got here—HI! This book has been a dream project for me since I was ten, because around that time my body started doing all these weird new things and I had so many questions and not enough answers. Twenty years later I feel like I have some of it figured out, so I wanted to put it all together and share it with you. This book is designed so you can dip in and out, and includes a whole bunch of my own embarrassing stories!

I spent my teenage years in Melbourne, Australia, and when I was young, my mom encouraged me to do a lot of sports, which I LOVED, and that finally led me to do a circus arts degree in college! Since then, I've spent my life traveling around as an international show girl, and now I work with young women through my hula-hooping troupe, The Majorettes.

But don't get me wrong, it's not all glamour. I still get my period at awkward moments and, occasionally, have to deal with unsinkable poops. For every one of us, sometimes something happens that is so weird you would think it is A) too embarrassing to ever mention or B) surely the only time it's ever happened in the history of womankind. But we have all been there! And despite this, I am still 100 percent convinced that being a girl is the BEST! Our bodies are AMAZING—and capable of doing lots of spectacular things.

It's a great time to be female—you only need to do a little research to know that womankind has had a pretty rough run through history. Now in the twenty-first century, we are crusading and breaking down stereotypes everywhere. You can do ANYTHING you want with your life! Go to the moon! Start an organic toothbrush company! Have a million babies! Hormones may be annoying till you work them out, but once you do, life can be just as fun as ever. KNOWLEDGE IS POWER. Get to know how your body works and how to make it work for you.

Go forth, little sister,
Marawa xo

Hi, I'm Marawa!

This was me at ten.

This is me now.

1

ALL EYES ON YOU

• • • • •

When you start looking like a little lady, people might start treating you like a woman. Boys and men might look at you differently, which can be nice or not-so-nice (see the "That Was Weird" chapter). And everyone else—friends, moms, the lady at your favorite corner store—might talk to you differently, too. This can be uncomfortable, especially if they say something about your body while you are just getting used to your new shape yourself. You don't want someone pointing out that you have boobs or that you've put on weight. I remember my friend's mom coming over to our house once and announcing in front of everyone that I had put on "so much weight, gosh!" and I was looking "so round"! My friend was even more embarrassed than me, I think— I just thought it was kind of annoying. I mean, I wasn't trying to make my body look different, it was doing that on its own!

Clothes
that used to fit were
suddenly really tight or
too short. Sometimes it
was fun and I was excited about being
bigger and stronger. Other times I wanted it to
stop so I could just stay the same forever.

I had younger brothers and sisters so I was
always desperate to be included among the
adults instead of the kids. But when things began
to change and I was no longer lumped in with
the kids ("oh the kids are outside;" "the kids are
watching TV"), suddenly adults were asking me
questions and wanting my opinions on things.
In some ways this was
great and made me feel
grown-up, but I was also
confused about what the
right thing to say was. I
suddenly felt overwhelmed.
I wanted to give the right answer
to every question—the smart
answer. But often I would feel

12

uncomfortable and in the
spotlight, or find myself
going along with conversa-
tions I didn't fully understand. It
was a weird feeling, realizing that
the "invisible kid" label was starting to dissolve.

All of this can be really frus-
trating and annoying. Sometimes you feel as
if you're being treated like a child and then,
when people start treating you like an adult, the
responsibility that comes with it can
seem unfair! My advice? Don't feel
in a rush to join the adult table!
You can take your time—it's nice
to be able to float between
adultland and kidsville for a while.

2

BOOBS, BREASTS, BRAS

• • • • •

Boobs are great! Once you get used to them . . .

Some grow bit by bit; some seem to appear overnight. Big or small, they are not going away, so embrace your breasts and look after them.

My friend's boobs really hurt when they were growing and felt hot and itchy—she was always afraid of people knocking into her chest, so she walked around with her arms crossed over it.

Mine appeared like balloons: one minute I was flat, the next they were there! Or that's how it felt. I liked them, but suddenly running, jumping, and all the things I loved doing became a lot harder. I hated it! I wanted to be able to jump up and down without this extra weight literally dragging me down.

My mom bought me the ugliest sports bra I had ever seen. I hated the look of it so much, but it did hold me in place and allow me to run the

← My first ugly sports bra

way I wanted to, so I wore it. BUT I put a cuter, less supportive sports bra on top and prayed that no one would see the monster straps of the nuclear warheads holding my boobs in place.

Full cup

These days I wear different bras for different occasions, but while your boobs are growing, it's best (and most comfortable) to get non-wired bras without too many odds 'n' ends. Also,

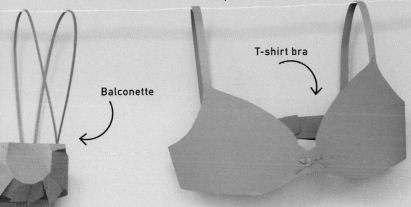

Balconette

T-shirt bra

different shapes suit different shapes! Try on a LOT before you buy— one size does NOT fit all.

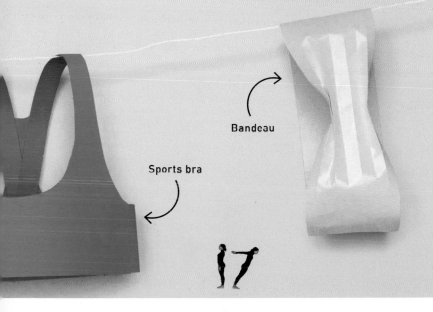

Bandeau

Sports bra

17

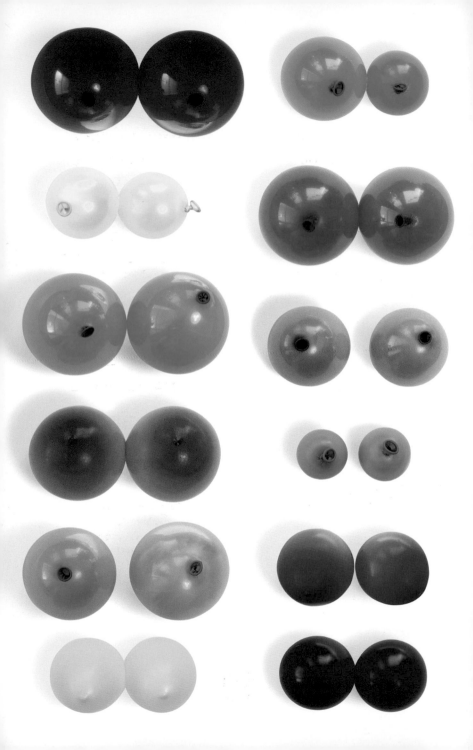

Most important, get your bra fitted. I had a friend in high school whose bra straps were always falling off her shoulders; she didn't realize you could actually tighten them! Guessing your own size can mean you get it wrong and have to put up with lots of discomfort: straps that are too tight, clasps digging into you, scratchy lace—ugghh . . . My boobs changed size every year, so it's worth getting fitted regularly, especially when you're still growing. And just remember that the bra-fitting lady sees boobs ALL DAY, so your new boobs are only new to you.

Also, it is COMPLETELY NORMAL to have:

One boob much bigger than the other

Stretch marks

Big, sticky-outy nipples

Tiny nipples that only pop out when you're cold

Blue veins

Hair, freckles, and moles

Boobs pointing in different directions

Oh, and . . . lots of other stuff. If you're unsure about ANYTHING, you can always ask your doctor.

3

DOT-TO-DOT

• • • • •

Changes in your body's hormones often produce . . . pimples! I managed to get through my teenage years with barely any, but then my skin started really breaking out in my twenties. Zits can break out on your face, your chest, your back, and even your bottom! DON'T TOUCH 'EM—it's just gonna make 'em worse. The best thing is to keep them oil free. Try using a very gentle cleanser (not soap) to wipe away oil, sweat, and dirt from air pollution. I use dots of a clay mask on pimples overnight to dry them out, and clear witch-hazel salve during the day (which is antiseptic, too). If your zits are really painful or won't go away, you may have acne. It's annoying, but it can be treated and you don't have to suffer. Get a parent to make an appointment with a doctor for you.

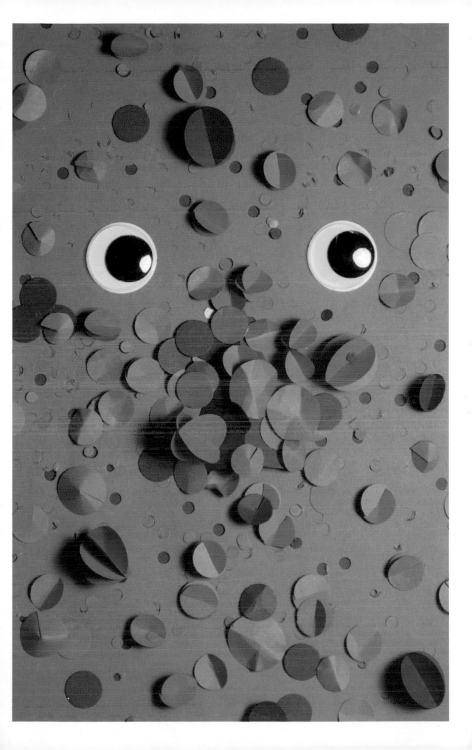

Don't panic! You might despair, but don't let zits ruin your week. Take a deep breath and remember this is temporary.

Zits hurt! Ice or a cold wash-cloth will soothe them. If a zit explodes, get some antiseptic on there so it doesn't get infected.

Cleanse! If you're having a breakout, clean your skin twice a day. Remember: Don't use regular soap—it's too harsh.

Drink tons! Water's so good for your body. It flushes out all the toxins and is great for your skin—keep glugging!

Avoid sugar! Cutting down on soft drinks and sugary snacks is healthier all around and should really help your skin.

No squeezing! It's so tempting, I know, but I promise this will just make them worse. Keep them clean and dry, and try not to touch!

Stand back! Zits always feel waaay bigger than they are. Stand away from the mirror to look at them. See? Much better!

Blackheads mean your skin's "breathing holes" are blocked with dirt. Taking care of your skin is the best way to avoid them.

4

BRACE FACE

· · · · ·

I had braces. If you don't have them, you probably know a friend who does. I didn't want them; I was convinced that I would kiss someone and we would get stuck together and have to go to the hospital and a reporter would take our picture and we would end up in the paper as "The World's Stupidest Teenagers." (I hadn't actually kissed anyone by this stage.)

Braces can be painful. After all, rearranging the teeth in your face is no small feat! BUT, if you are lucky enough to get them, be grateful. Straight teeth are a luxury and are with you for life. At the time, being a brace face felt like a life sentence to me, but now it feels like it was barely a moment. Though, admittedly, every time I bite into an apple, I am so happy I don't have to spend an hour picking it out of my teeth.

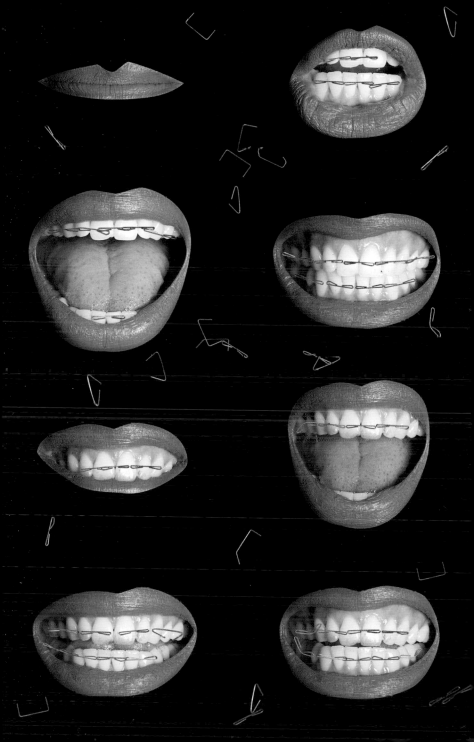

5

SWEAT . . . LIKE A GIRL!

• • • • •

Newsflash: men, women, girls, and boys sweat. There's no way around it—just like all human beings, YOU'VE GOTTA SWEAT! Whether it's from exercise, excitement, heat, or anger, your body sweats to help cool you down. But sometimes with sweat comes a smell, and often we want to try to disguise it. I remember telling my mom that I needed deodorant—I smelled like sweat and I didn't want to. I was sure everyone on the train could smell me. What I didn't realize was that even if it's strong, your body's natural smell is actually often pleasant to other people, so long as it is FRESH! But I thought I should smell like an air freshener: I wanted the smell of roses to come out of me. So, I got deodorant. But there are things I wish I'd known . . .

First, there are deodorants and there are anti-perspirants. Deodorants simply mask your body odor; they don't stop sweating. Antiperspirants, on the other hand, have aluminum in them—you can see it listed in the ingredients. Aluminum blocks sweat from coming out of your pores.

This is:

GOOD

because the sweat stops, so you stay dry under your arms.

BAD

because sweat is your body's natural way of cooling itself down. Doctors advise that aluminum is not meant to be rubbed all over your skin! You can get natural deodorants that don't have aluminum—BUT—they are less effective at covering the smell of sweat.

So it's a tricky decision. But there are other things you can do to combat sweat and odor!

Like I said, the smell of sweat isn't actually unpleasant when it's fresh. Sometimes I really like it! To keep fresh, here are some tips:

Showers

It sounds obvious, but make sure you wash really well every day, with soap! Get in under your armpits and scrub!

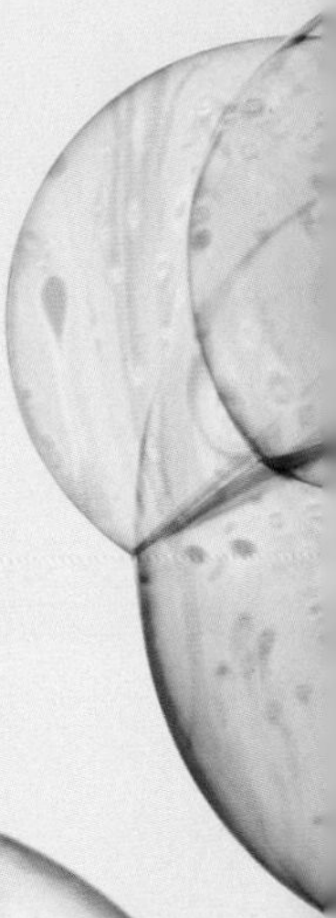

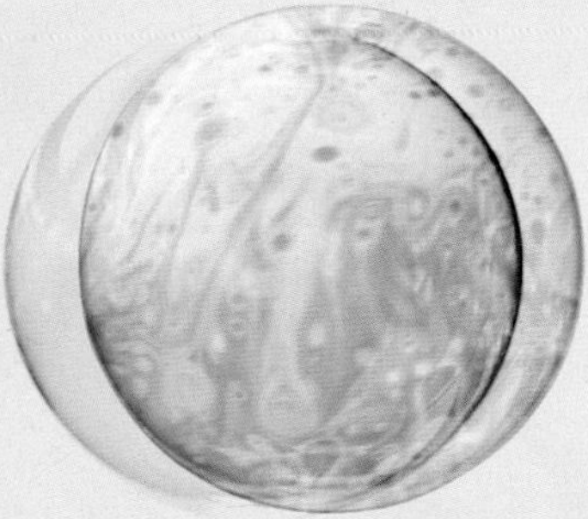

Natural deodorant

BEFORE you get sweaty, use a natural deodorant on your clean skin. You can reapply during the day if you really feel like you need to— I sometimes do if I work out and get sweaty—but it's your call. Some people love the smell of their own sweat. BREATHE DEEP!

Clothes

This one is really
important. Natural fibers,
like cotton or wool, allow your
skin to breathe. Synthetic fabrics,
like polyester or acrylic, don't. They
just lock the heat in like plastic
wrap. It makes a huge difference
to the sweat situation, so
always read the label.

6

YOU ARE NOT ALONE

. . . . .

. . . even though sometimes it really, REALLY feels like you are. I used to have two types of feeling alone. One was when there was a party and EVERYONE in the world was going and my dad would not let me go (this was a theme for most of my high school years). I would be so mad and feel like the whole world was turning but no one knew or cared that I existed. Sitting at home, bored, in my room with nothing to do . . . ugghh. It was the worst.

The other type of alone would just come out of nowhere: All of a sudden, I would feel like nothing made sense and the world was a huge place and I was lost in a giant universe. I knew deep down that I had friends and people loved me, but in that moment, right then, I just felt really alone—like nobody understood what I was feeling or thinking about, and nobody cared about

me. I could usually snap out of this by talking myself back to logicland or calling a friend or writing in a journal. Sometimes you've just got to get all those thoughts out and then everything feels normal again.

There are plenty of other emotions that kicked in when I was in high school. Feeling awkward—so awkward that even saying hello to someone seemed like an obstacle course I was sure to fail. Was it "hi," "hey," "wassaaaaap," a hug, high five, or a wave? And then I'd end up making some weird squeaking sound that was definitely not cool. Feeling embarrassed, especially in public, was THE WORST. Although I can't even remember what I was embarrassed about (which shows how pointless it was), I do remember spending days agonizing over embarrasing moments and playing them again and again in my mind.

I wish I could have not stressed about these things and moved on, but maybe that's all part of the process. These days, I embarrass myself regularly but I don't let it bother me . . . I guess I just needed more practice.

37

7

WITNESS THE FITNESS

· · · · ·

Being active is essential to a healthy lifestyle. But getting motivated to move can be almost harder than the exercise itself! Overcoming self-consciousness is also a huge hurdle. I remember when I began getting heavier, I would think and think about starting to exercise but never quite get around to doing it. . . . I always had a good excuse! I wanted to be perfect at everything—or at least good at it—so learning a new sport or anything that made me feel vulnerable, or potentially laughed at, had a huge DON'T GO THERE sticker on it.

But if you are going to look after your body, you need to get that heart rate UP UP UP, and you need to sweat. Not only is exercise great for you long-term, but short-term you get a rush of endorphins, which are the feel-good chemicals released into your brain that make you

feel happy and good about yourself. What's not to like?

The only question left is: Which kind of exercise do I pick? Personally, I find many types of exercise B-O-R-I-N-G. It's so important to find something that you actually enjoy! OBVIOUSLY I am biased but I think hula-hooping is the most fun exercise ever. And also roller-skating, jumping rope, and dancing like I am on *Soul Train*. But there are many other things out there—you just need to find your groove. If you consider exercising a real chore, you can work it into your week by setting a goal to do twenty minutes, three times a week. It's easy to find time if you plan ahead—twenty minutes first thing in the morning is a great way to begin the day! If you need a little head start, you can also exercise in private before unleashing your new skills on the world! But try not to feel too self-conscious. Everyone knows you have to start at the start— even champions were beginners once. Sports are a great way to build confidence. The hardest part is taking that first step!

8

HIGH HEELS, ARE YOU FOR REAL?

· · · · ·

I was seventeen when I got my first pair of heels. I loved the look and idea of them but did NOT like the pain in the balls of my feet. Heels also stop you from moving freely—so, as a young person, there's no WAY I would wear them! Your bones 'n' joints are still growing, and wearing heels can throw everything out of alignment. Heels are terrible for your posture and back. Your bones are not yet fully formed! On average, girls' bones stop growing between the ages of fourteen and fifteen—this is when bones stop being bendy and have a lower risk of being thrown out of joint. So at the very least, wait till then. And heels are great for a couple of hours at a time, but not during the day when you're running around. If I go out in heels, I make sure I have a pair of flats with me, too.

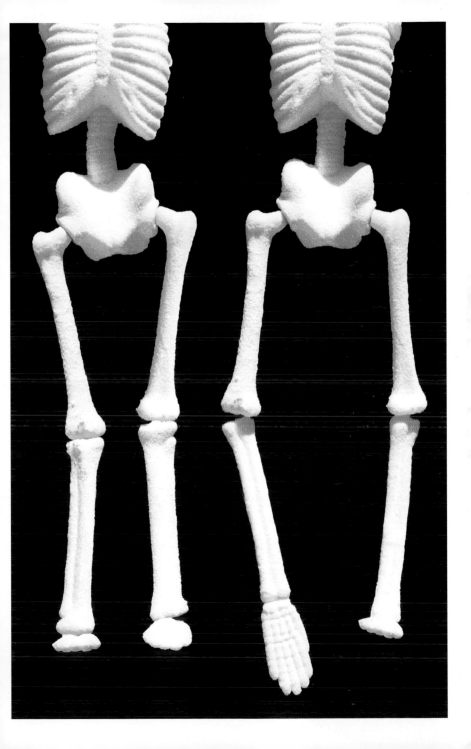

THE PEE STORY

• • • • •

When I was fourteen, I wet my pants.

It was a normal day. I walked home—in my sports uniform—and, as per usual, as soon as I saw the house I needed to pee. This still happens to me now—when I get home I immediately need to pee. Anyway, on this particular day I didn't have a key, which was fine because there was a spare around the back. Except, there wasn't. Still, no problem—I knew how to climb in through the upstairs bedroom window. So I climbed onto the roof. And for the first time in the history of my house, all the windows were locked. Now I was getting annoyed. This was before cell phones, so I couldn't call my family to see who was nearby, and I was too embarrassed to ask the neighbors. I sat in the backyard trying to come up with a plan. I really, REALLY needed to pee. I lay on my back, thinking that might help. Then I propped my legs up against the wall. That made it worse. I started getting shooting pains. I thought about sit-ups and how strong my stomach was and how I should be able to hold it in. I thought about squatting down somewhere and just peeing, but then I kept thinking someone would hear me and look over the fence and see my vagina and I would DIE of embarrassment.

So I squeezed and squeezed, cursing every single one of my family members for not leaving a window open or a key out. Then . . . I felt a little trickle start. *Oh my God, this was happening.* I went and stood under the clothesline and silently wet my undies. And my sweatpants. And my socks. And my shoes—which I kicked off almost in time. It was warm and unstoppable, and it must have been a whole liter. I was mortified. And then cold. I took a pair of my mom's pajama pants off the clothesline and then silently and awkwardly peeled out of my wet sweatpants and into her pajamas, which stuck to my legs since they weren't dry. OMG, the horror. Literally as I was putting them on, I heard my mom's car pull into the driveway. I STORMED out to inform her that she was the worst mother ever for not leaving me a key. But when I got out front she was talking to a girl from my school who was walking past. They both looked at me, standing there in pajama pants and half a sports uniform. I said, "Oh, hi," and then helped her unpack the car, like everything was fine. Worst day ever.

VAGINA

• • • • •

So, when you learn about your vagina, you find out that you have a hole going up inside you, behind your pee hole, that you can stick your finger right up. I thought that was SO WEIRD! Where was the end? Was there an end? What else was up there? What about when I go swimming? Does the water go up there—DOES IT COME BACK OUT? AM I DRINKING THAT WATER?! (The answers are: your cervix; yes; your womb, fallopian tubes, and other stuff; what about it?; probably; probably; probably!) I don't think I sat and actually LOOKED at my vagina till I was about fourteen because it kind of grossed me out—there was hair and a new smell and all sorts of things happening. Was this the unique, special thing everyone made it out to be?

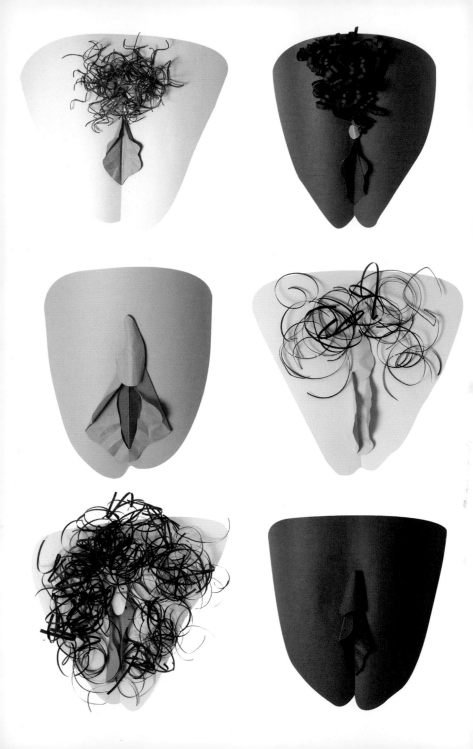

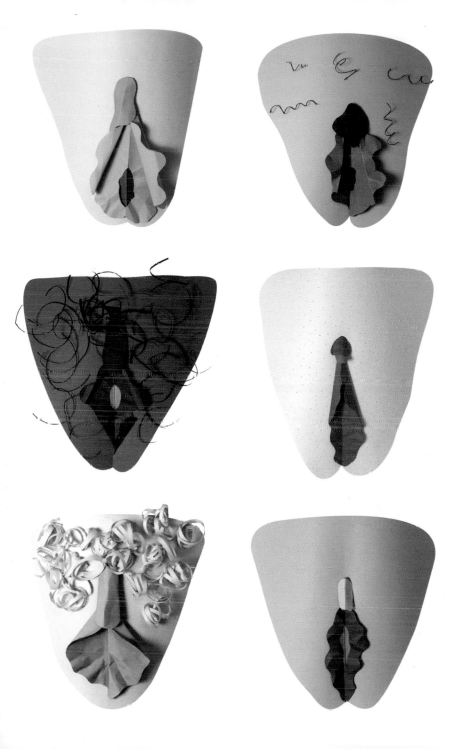

Eventually I locked the bathroom door and got out a mirror to see exactly what was going on. It looked complicated—messy and unfamiliar. After a lot of searching through medical books, I discovered that I was not the only person in the world with this crazy-looking, hairy clamshell—I was just like every other woman out there. This complex creation we all own is often compared to a delicate and intricate flower (which I like) and since it wasn't going anywhere, I went about identifying all the parts and finding out how they worked. I discovered which bit was the clitoris (for pleasure) and which part was the urethra (pee hole). I even managed the complicated task of holding a mirror between my legs while I peed, to make sure that everything was where it was meant to be according to the anatomy guides. Luckily it was—a relief, as I was always worried that something was going to be out of order and embarrassing.

Nowadays I don't know why we women are sometimes embarrassed about talking about our vaginas. Boys are proud of their private parts! Maybe it's because ours go in and theirs go out.

I remember when I was six I thought it was so unfair that boys could pee easily wherever they were, while girls couldn't. I was convinced that if I trained myself, I could learn how to make my pee shoot out in an arc, too. I decided to give it a try. I stood a good yard away from the toilet, curled my little hips under, and thrust my pee forward, waiting for my triumphant stream to land on target in the toilet. To my horror, I immediately felt the hot sensation of it running down my leg and into my pants around my ankles. Disappointed, I let my mom believe I'd had an accident. I tried this at least five more times until I admitted defeat and felt sad about my inability to project my pee. To this day, I've never managed to get my pee to fly! (Still trying.)

Anyway, just remember: Your foo foo is your friend. You will be together for life, so get to know her! KNOWLEDGE IS POWER! As soon as I felt like I knew exactly what was going on down there, I felt more confident and in control of my own body.

Here it is in all its inner glory! This diagram is EVERYTHING you need to know about your VAGIIIIIIINA! You've seen already that vaginas come in lots of different shapes, colors, and sizes, but whatever yours looks like, it'll be made up of these parts.

And, an important note before we continue: While "vagina" has become the most commonly used word for referring to women's genitalia, "vulva" is actually the correct medical term for all of the external organs, including the pubic mound, labia, important clitoris, and the external openings of the urethra *and* vagina.

INNER LABIA
"Labia" just means "lips" in Latin. These lips surround your vagina and urethra to protect them and keep them clean, moist, and healthy.

OUTER LABIA
These lips form the opening to your genitals and surround your clitoris and inner lips, protecting and enclosing them.

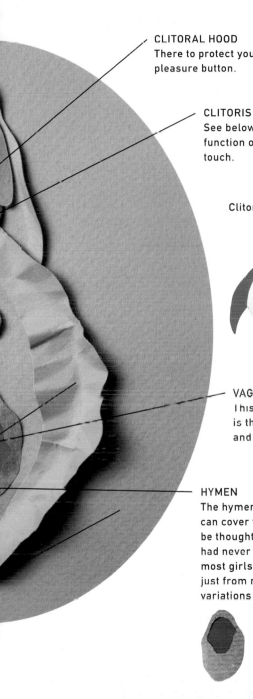

CLITORAL HOOD
There to protect your personal pleasure button.

CLITORIS
See below for what it looks like inside. The function of this organ is to feel ticklish to the touch.

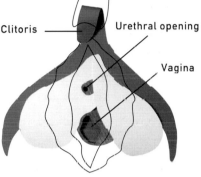

Clitoris —

Urethral opening

Vagina

VAGINA
This is the passage to your womb. This is the hole your period comes out from and from where babies are born.

HYMEN
The hymen is a very thin membrane of skin that can cover the opening to the vagina. It used to be thought that a complete hymen "proved" you had never had sex, but that's nonsense since most girls stretch it open when they're young just from running around. It can look like variations on any of these:

WHAT'S THE WHITE STUFF?

• • • • •

Whitish, yellowish stuff in your undies is 100 percent normal. When I first got it, I was convinced it meant there was something wrong with me. But nothing is wrong with me or with you, trust me! A healthy vagina is a moist vagina and some of that moistness gets on your underwear—that's it. Sometimes, once you start getting your period, you may notice this discharge looks more like a clearish jelly (actually, like egg whites!). This means that you are ovulating: Your body has released a tiny egg and is making a nice little jelly cushion in your womb for it to land in. (I won't tell you all about how ovulation and periods work here—it's a lot to explain.) Sometimes that jelly just appears in my undies out of nowhere, and sometimes I can feel it and I think I'm getting my period. It's weird but you get used to it! You can track it the same way you can track your period, since it runs on the same cycle. I started putting mine into a period tracker app, which made it really easy to predict. But when you first get your period, it can be all over the place, so don't stress—just be prepared. A bit of everyday vaginal discharge is completely normal. The only time you want to investigate is if the consistency is a bit chunkier and there is a lot of it, or if it has a really strong smell—this can be a symptom of a yeast infection (which is treatable—see our chapter on page 198).

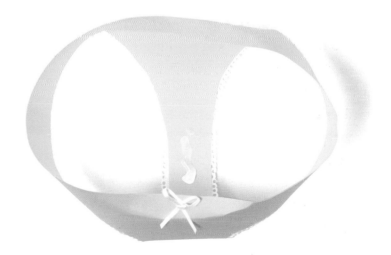

12

HAIRAPY

• • • • •

Hair is weird. We can spend so much time banishing it from some parts of our body and then hours looking after it on other parts. And hair is magical: I have a friend who has reealllly long hair and she can actually hang from it—it's her performance specialty and it's called a hair suspension. Totally crazy! Apart from being strong enough to hang from, our hair can also have a big effect on how we feel. A new haircut or style can make you feel like a whole new person!

I've had so much fun with my hair—I think I've done everything to it: bleached it, braided it, dyed it, henna'd it. Straightened it, tied it up, slicked it back, combed it out, and eventually, when nothing was left, shaved it all off (I just did it again during the making of this book, in fact)! Shaving it was cool—I felt like I was having

my own personal protest against the world of "appearance is everything." People spend so much energy worrying about how they look or what other people think of them. And the time it took to comb, style, and look after a full head of hair . . . I was on a mission to LIVE LIFE and spending seven or more hours a week combing and styling was not part of my plan!

So my message to you is: it's JUST HAIR—it will grow back. GO NUTS, I say—EXPERIMENT. Just know that if you suddenly realize you made a terrible mistake with a home dyeing kit, or if a pair of scissors and a song made you get a little lost in the moment—it's not forever! Embrace a haircut gone wrong and make it work for you. Add some clips, a turban, a headband, beanie, hat, or wig—whatever! One day—maybe not in the near future—but one day, you will look back on that picture and laugh and laugh (and maybe remember how you cried and cried) and that will be your hair making you feel good again—hairapy rules!

13

HAIR, THERE, EVERYWHERE!

• • • • •

One minute your skin is nice and smooth, the next you notice that wispy hairs have appeared under your arms and between your legs—even on your upper lip or around your nipples! It can feel like you're turning into a gorilla.

I kind of loved all my new body hair and kind of hated it. At first I let it grow—it was really exciting, and a sign that I was starting to turn into a woman. But then I wanted to try taking it off, too, which was also exciting. I wanted to wax, but was scared it was going to hurt. Eventually I did it and it wasn't as bad as I thought it would be.

Nowadays, I think there are no rules.

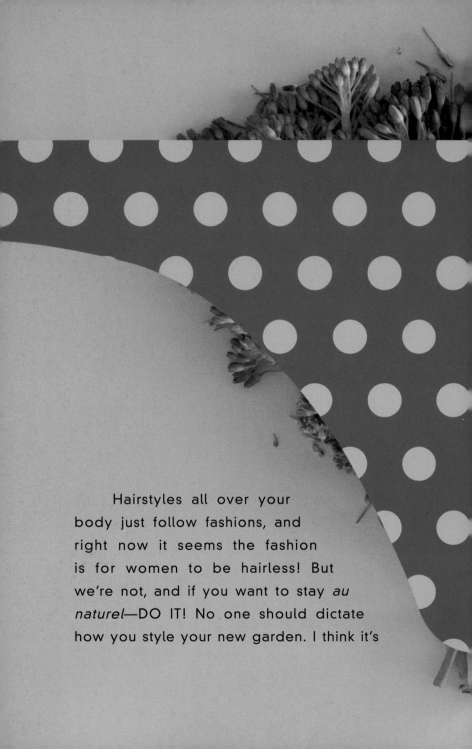

Hairstyles all over your body just follow fashions, and right now it seems the fashion is for women to be hairless! But we're not, and if you want to stay *au naturel*—DO IT! No one should dictate how you style your new garden. I think it's

beautiful, and there are lots of women all over the world who let their armpit and leg hair flourish, no matter what others are doing. If you do want to get rid of it, that's also fine—turn to page 134 for some hot tips.

14

JUST EAT IT

• • • • •

I ate a lot in high school. I figured I was growing and my body needed fuel! And grow it did . . . I stopped getting taller after I was about eleven, but kept filling out. And I loved it—except for the stretch marks, maybe. But my mom told me those would fade, so I just hoped they would (they did) and got on with it. For breakfast in my senior year of high school, I would some-times make a special sandwich and wash the whole thing down with a milkshake. Afterward, all I wanted to do was go back to bed. I don't recommend this as a daily habit. I DO, however, recommend trying this sandwich at least once so you know what I am talking about.

Marawa's triple toastie:
– 3 slices of wholegrain bread
– 2 slices of cheese
– 2 tbs of baked beans
– 2 tbs of canned spaghetti

Layer the bread and cheese. Put the beans on one side and put the spaghetti on the other. The hardest thing is getting it into the sandwich-maker but, once toasted, you are SET!

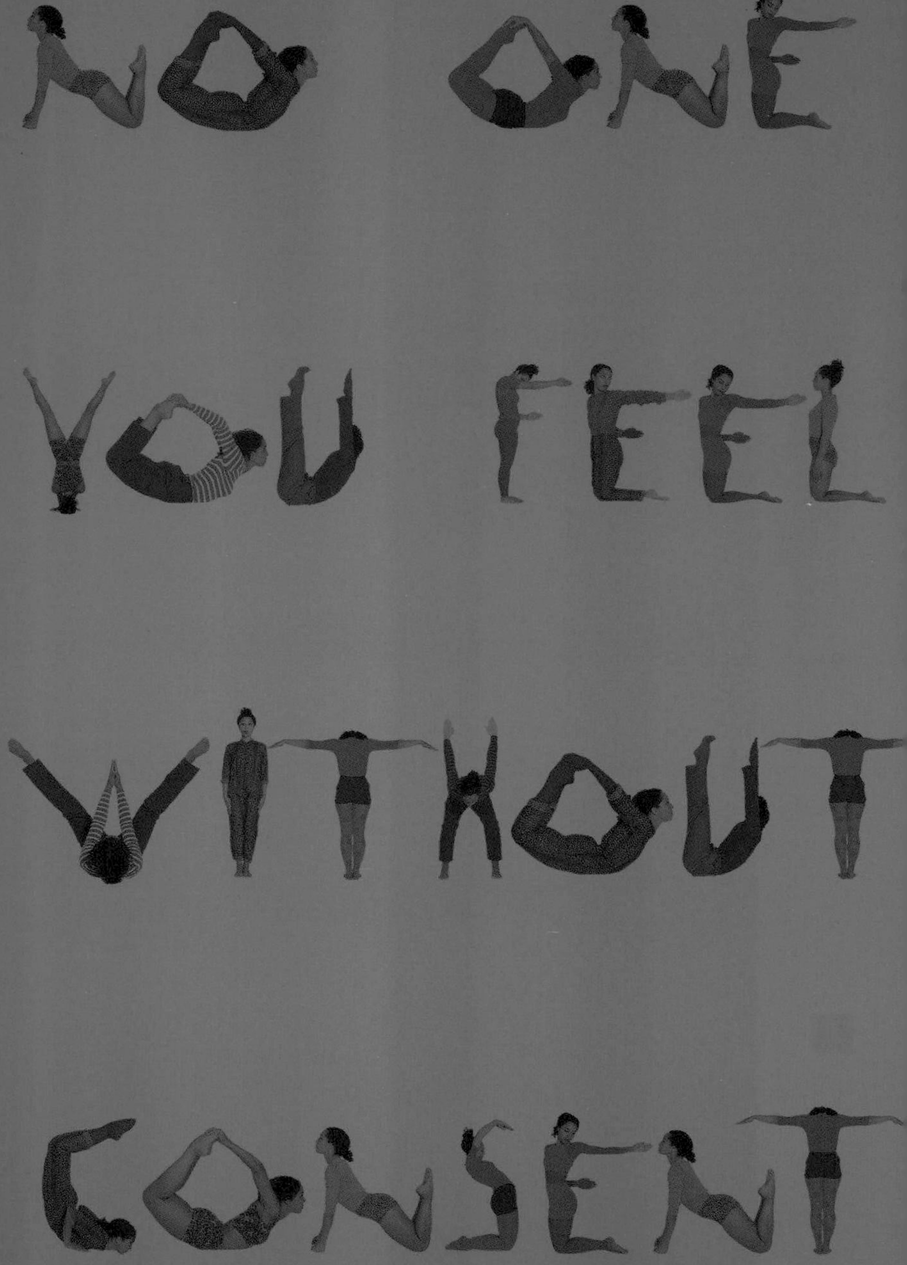

NO ONE

YOU FEEL

WITHOUT

CONSENT

CAN MAKE
INFERIOR
YOUR

— Eleanor Roosevelt

15

HEARTBREAK

• • • • •

UGH. Heartbreak HURTS. It hurts so bad you can feel like you want to dieee. But it passes—sometimes it feels like forever, but it definitely passes. Tough, tough times. I used to think it would actually hurt inside my heart, but it felt more like a dark cloud inside my whole body. I felt tired and heavy and I had no appetite. Everything was GRAY. No one could cheer me up and I was convinced this new state of monochrome was how I would live out my years. But eventually the clouds lifted and I was able to feel happy again. All the color of life returned and I was back to normal. The best thing to do is throw yourself into something you enjoy—play your favorite sport; see your friends; read your books. Whatever it is, I promise it'll speed up the healing process. Distraction and time is what you need. But I completely understand your pain. ♥

16

DANCE

• • • • •

. . . like nobody is watching! (Or, if you prefer, like everyone is watching!)

Sometimes a good dance can help even the biggest disaster, problem, or pain. There are so many types of dance out there—jazz, ballet, contemporary, hip-hop, country, salsa, tap, line, ballroom, tango, folk, break, vogue . . . SO MANY that you can take a dance class in just about anything!

A lot of dance relates to certain types of music, so that's sometimes a good way to figure out what you like. Music can bring everything out of you—tears, joy, anger, energy, calmness—and moving to it is an amazing way to express yourself. You may not like what's in the top 100, but find what works for you—there are so many great sounds out there. Experiment with the radio to discover what feeds your soul. And when you

discover it, put it on in your bedroom and dance it out! Get your headphones and prance around the park!

I will dance to just about anything if I like the song. I usually feel like the music takes over and I move according to what the song is doing. I LOVE watching people dance, too. Sometimes, the most unlikely people hear their favorite tune and get so into it. You can really see a story in people's movement! My mom LOSES it anytime she hears "I Will Survive" by Gloria Gaynor. She will drop whatever she is doing and she's off—singing, dramatic arm movements in the air, spins, jazz hands. It's a masterpiece! Just watching her do it makes me happy.

If you don't know where to start, stand or sit and listen to the music. Try shaking your arms around, bending your knees in time, or jumping. Not every dance needs to look like a slick music video—don't limit yourself! Find your inner dancing queen, whoever she is!

17

PERIODS: THE MYSTERY

• • • • •

Periods. Eventually they come to all of us, in various wondrous, bloody forms! Sometimes your period is heavy, sometimes light. Sometimes it comes and goes: a bit here, a bit there, nothing for a day and then it's back! But usually within a week you are safe to wear white underwear again without fear of any staining. I always need to pee more when I'm getting my period and I fart way more. Sorry, but it's true! And while I am being honest: I usually have a massive poop the day I get it. It's like my whole body is resetting, which is nice . . . like a monthly cleanse! Your period is a sign that you are becoming a woman. There is nothing to be scared about, other than perhaps being stranded without a spare tampon or pad! All women have had periods throughout history: famous women, athlete women, poor women, rich women—women of all religions

78

and all cultures in every part of the world. It's weird that we still don't hear all that much about periods—like they're something embarrassing. Thankfully, some cultures celebrate girls getting their periods, though unfortunately this is often linked to being ready for marriage and babies—which, if you still have plans for conquering the world as the best athlete, horse trainer, or astronaut, might not be what you had in mind!

There are plenty of people who are comfortable talking about periods, so don't be afraid to ask your friends and older girls or women. Like most things in life, with time and practice you learn how to handle this monthly visitor. More and more women are talking openly about their periods, sharing stories, experiences, and lifting the mystery behind our monthly cycle. HURRAH!

18

MY FIRST PERIOD

● ● ● ● ●

So: my mom was in the next room with some of her friends, while all their kids, me, and my brother and sister were watching TV. A commercial for sanitary pads came on, with a girl smiling and riding a bike while a cute animation showed how a pad with wings would stick to your undies. I remember thinking that riding a bike in half a diaper could NOT be comfortable.

A few minutes later, I suddenly felt like my pants were wet. Unlike my friends—most of whom found out when they went to the bathroom and found a little blood in their underwear—I knew what it was right away. Not to mention I'd just watched a winged pad fly around on TV! Weird timing . . .

I leapt up and hurried to the toilet, squeezing like I was trying not to pee—but it made no difference and I could feel the blood seeping into

my underwear. It didn't hurt at all—not like when you cut yourself and bleed. I just had a dull ache in my tummy. It felt so strange; I couldn't stop it, nor could I push it all out—my body wasn't listening to my commands.

Anyway, I sat there on the toilet trying to work out how to hide it. I really didn't want everyone to know what was going on inside my body—I wanted to deal with it myself first—but at that moment I felt very out of control. How much more blood would come? Was I going to have to sit on the toilet all night? There was no way around it—I needed my mom. I put a bunch of toilet paper in my pants and waddled out. She was sitting with her friends, chatting, and I called quietly to her from the doorway. She looked over at me, confused, and I said, "Mom! You need to come with me! Now!" and everyone stopped talking to look at me, which added to my already totally embarrassed state. She came, asking me what was going on, as I marched her all the way back to the bathroom. I told her I had my period and she said, "Oh—wow—oh!" way too loudly. I was SO EMBARRASSED. Then she asked me if I was sure. I showed her my pants and then she said, "Right, don't worry—I'll be back." She went to the drugstore and returned with a huge bag of sanitary pads. Anyway, she showed me what to do and said I might want to put TWO in that night so that I could sleep without leaking, in case the flow stayed heavy. TWO?! These things felt ENORMOUS! I remember thinking, *This is my life now!* Ugh!

So that was my first period, forever unforgettable. It felt very strange and unfamiliar. Until then, I had felt the same as the boys I played with. Now, here was something that made me different. There was no way back and that was a weird feeling, like growing up overnight. But after all the initial panics and thoughts wore off, it got a lot better and easier! Tampons and pads went from feeling huge to being tiny things I didn't even notice. What had felt awkward and scary became more predictable and easy to deal with, and I learned to really appreciate how amazing my body is! Lots of girls' periods can take a couple of years to become regular. Usually, they settle down, but if they don't, or if they're very heavy or painful, it's worth seeing your doctor, who will be able to help.

19

OWN YOUR PERIOD

• • • • •

Periods get a bad rap. From being called "the curse" to whispered comments about your "time of the month," it can seem like people only talk in a negative way about the exaggerated feelings your period can bring on. But I think there are lots of things to enjoy about your period.

In the days leading up to mine, I can feel sort of swollen all over and a bit hot. Then, when it first comes, I often get cramps in my abdomen and feel like my vagina is achy or swollen inside and out. Also, I get the occasional weird, shooty butt pain, like a muscle twitch—so weird! The cramps are annoying but I quite enjoy having a hot water bottle strapped to me and snuggling up with a cup of tea. I also have this unraveling kind of sensation, like all the tension

is leaving me. Often, halfway through my period, I feel like everything is a bit new and calm, like I'm resetting.

I used to feel really lucky to be a girl EXCEPT for periods—I thought they were so messy and gross. Having to carry tampons was annoying and it felt unfair to have to factor my period into things I did.

Now I feel lucky to get it!

One thing I love about it is that my mind goes into a very productive place—I am hyper-aware of smells, sounds, and touch. Things taste different—sweeter or spicier than usual—and I crave certain foods, especially potatoes. I love potatoes. . . . The day I get my period is also my most creative: I try to draw, write, or make something on that day because my mind goes to interesting places. If I'm feeling crampy, I do some stretches or go for a walk and listen to music—everything sounds good! I also feel extra-emotional—a commercial on TV can make me cry—but a really good cry is such a cleansing experience! Afterward, you gather yourself up, wash your face, and get back to it. You feel clearer in your mind as well as in your sinuses. And crying like that doesn't mean you're unhappy.

Getting my period lets me know my body is running smoothly. I like the monthly feeling of being very aware of myself. And I love how periods are something that bond women—we all experience the same thing and can compare notes and connect over this totally female phenomenon. Periods can feel like they are getting in the way of life, but if you acknowledge what's happening, try to plan ahead, and gain knowledge, you can really use your period to your advantage! Listen to your body and learn as you go. Each period gives you an opportunity to see what works best for you. Don't be ruled by your period—own it.

20

SANITARY SANITY

• • • • •

In the beginning . . . women created sanitary pads. But they weren't the self-adhesive, super-absorbent, cutely wrapped versions we know today. First, we had to go through all kinds of fun: for centuries, rags that were washed and reused were the most common, though women all over the world have had to resort to putting dirt and even sand in undergarments to catch their periods. Then, around the end of the nineteenth century, the sanitary belt arrived. It was literally a long towel that looped into hoops at the front and back on a belt around your waist. But this moved around all the time and was uncomfortable. Finally, some genius put adhesive on the underside of a much smaller pad and—VOILÀ!— the modern pad was born. Pad technology is always improving—pads are thinner and more absorbent than ever. Now, sometimes they're even incorporated into the crotch of regular underwear—you can just wear . . . and wash!

Throughout the world, pads are still the most common method of absorbing our monthly magic. The first few days of my period are usually pretty heavy so I prefer to use tampons, but for those lighter days it's nice to have all these different options! I usually switch to a panty liner (a thin pad) or the all-in-one undies.

And know this: All of us, many times, have had to roll up toilet paper to make an emergency pad. And it always—without fail—works its way up the back of your underwear as you walk. And sometimes even out the top. It's okay! We've all been there!

Pad checklist:

- Keep one or two handy: the emergency pad in my bag has saved me many times!
- Work out how to stick it in the middle of your underwear—which is usually right over the crotch. At night, if you sleep on your back, you will want to stick it farther back (and vice versa for front/side sleeping). Or try a night-time pad—they are longer!
- Dispose of them properly! Wrap the old one up in toilet paper or the wrapper of your next pad and make sure it is fully in the trash can, rather than sticking to the lid! Also, never flush them—no one wants a clogged toilet and no one wants to swim in the ocean with your used pad. Trust me.
- Just like tampons and menstrual cups (more on those in a sec), you need to change your pad regularly—usually a few times a day, depending on how heavy your flow is and how absorbent the pad is.

PROS:	CONS:
• You can see everything, and know when you need to change.	• They can chafe and feel uncomfortable! You can't forget you're on your period like with tampons and menstrual cups.
• Nothing to learn—tampons and menstrual cups take a bit of practice, so pads are a great place to start.	• You can't swim—and I love swimming!
	• Sometimes, the sticky back catches on your pubic hair. Ouch!

21

TAMPONS: THE THINGS ON THE STRINGS

• • • • •

I used to think that tampons just kind of sat outside of you longways, between your labia—like a pad without the sticky part. I was SO HORRIFIED when I found out they had to go INSIDE you—I could not wrap my head around it. It seemed messy and dirty and gross. When I finally got my period, I tried pads but I couldn't deal with them—I was always leaking and it felt like a giant surfboard in my pants. So I spent a whole afternoon jamming tampons up inside me to try them out. At first I only put each one JUST inside me—I didn't understand that you had to push it up farther, and anyway, I was worried it would go up and not come back out. But it was soooo uncomfortable . . . I walked around with it grating inside me and it felt horrible. Eventually I

worked out that if you push it up higher then you won't be able to feel it anymore. Hurrah! Also, even if the string accidentally goes up, too, you can still get to it. Once I worked tampons out I never looked back: I was free to easily go swimming, running, jumping—everything!

Interesting fact: Even though womankind has done well fighting for equality over the years, there is such a thing as a "tampon tax"—proof that we still have a bit of work to do. Tampons (and all sanitary products, like pads and menstrual cups) are classed by many governments as "luxury" items. In other words, they're something you want but don't really *need*, and so we have to pay more for them. Excuse me? In what way are sanitary products nonessential items? This drives me CRAZY! There have been so many discussions about removing the tax, but as I write these words, women still have to pay to have periods. Unbelievable.

95

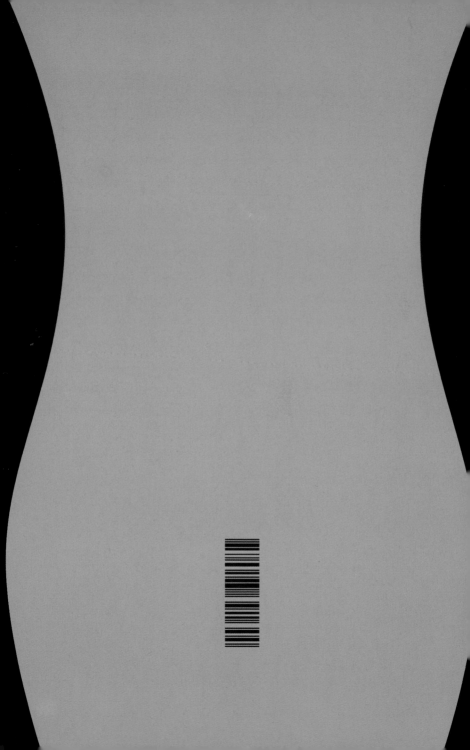

Tampon checklist:

- Don't leave it in too long and do read the packaging to make sure you're using the right size. It's possible (but highly unlikely) that you might get a reaction to it, called Toxic Shock Syndrome.
- Try to buy natural ones. A number of tampons contain things other than plain cotton. Read the labels and ask!
- Carry spares in a cute little bag or purse. You can easily disguise them so they don't fall out everywhere when you take out your wallet.
- Help your fellow sister. I have been saved by, or helped, many a girl with a spare tampon when a period turned up—especially at first, when your cycle can be a bit of a mystery!
- Don't flush them—just like pads, you need to dispose of them in the trash.

PROS:	CONS:
● You can swim!	● If you don't change your tampon in time, you can leak into your undies.
● You can't feel it once it has been inserted properly, unlike a pad.	● They take a little practice to get used to.
● They're small and easy to carry around.	● If your flow is too light to soak into the whole tampon, it can grate when you pull it out.

22

CUP O'

· · · · ·

Menstrual cups are not as well known as tampons and pads, but are becoming super popular because they are reusable and environmentally friendly. A menstrual cup is small and made of latex rubber—you kind of fold it in on itself and then insert it into your vagina. Once inside, it pops open and is held there by the walls of your vagina. It creates a cup that catches the blood rather than soaking it up like a tampon would. Then, when you want to change it, you pull it out by the nozzle at the bottom, tip it into the toilet bowl, rinse it, and pop it back in again. It can take a while to get used to, but there are plenty of tutorials online that show how to insert one, and once you've got the hang of it, you and your menstrual cup can go anywhere and everywhere together!

Menstrual cup checklist:

Get a size that works for you—the first one I tried was too big and I couldn't get comfortable at all! You may need to try different brands.

Even though it holds three times as much liquid as a tampon, you are still supposed to empty it out every four to six hours. You need to make sure your hands are really clean when using your menstrual cup.

It's one of the trickier things to get the hang of, so read up and learn as much as you can through other people's stories first.

Read the cup's cleaning instructions carefully.

PROS:	CONS:
• You only have to buy it once! No more running to the store because you're out of tampons/pads. Also because of this, it's super eco friendly!	• It can be messy! Especially if it is quite full—you need to really practice removing the cup a few times to be able to do it neatly.
• It holds a lot of flow so you can leave it in a little longer than a tampon and—like a tampon—you can't feel a thing. So you can completely forget you have your period all day.	• It can be difficult to empty out in a public toilet because you need to wash your hands and rinse the cup. The trick is to take a bottle of water in the stall with you.
• You see everything! Emptying a menstrual cup is an amazing insight into what is going on inside your body! A lot of girls have made art using their menstrual blood to create amazing pictures.	• It's tricky to insert at first. It requires a bit of practice to get the fold and insertion right. But once you've got it, you'll never look back!

THE LEAK STORY

• • • • •

When I first got my period, I read everything I could about this new mystery thing. One of the lessons I "learned" (and later found to be completely useless) is that periods run on a twenty-eight day cycle—so I marked down a huge red P every twenty-eighth day in my diary and thought that was taken care of. A couple of months later, we went out for a day trip with another family. There were lots of kids, including a teenage boy the same age as me. We had a great day out and then everyone piled back in the cars to go home again. A few of the kids wanted to travel together in one car. So I was wedged between my brother and this other boy my age, and I suddenly real-

102

ized I was getting my period. I was horrified. Not only did we have a loooong car ride ahead of us, but because I thought this was a day I was NOT SUPPOSED to get my period, I dressed that morning in my white denim overalls. Can you believe it? With an orange tie-dyed T-shirt, if I remember correctly. I panicked and clenched my legs hard, trying to stop any blood from coming out of me. But every now and then I felt it trickling out, no matter how hard I squeezed! I was trying to act like nothing was happening and laughed away. But that only made it worse—every time I laughed I felt more coming out. At one point I casually looked down to try to check between my legs and see if it was real or if it was all in my mind (y'know, the way you think it's everywhere when actually it's just a tiny spot on your underwear?) and, good gracious, there was UNDENIABLE, BRIGHT, RED-AS-RED BLOOD SOAKING THROUGH MY WHITE-AS-WHITE DENIM OVERALLS!

Then a new panic set in—what about the seat? Was it all over the seat? Did it smell? I was horrified at the thought that this boy was going to see it. I felt so exposed and gross. I just figured I had to keep my legs as tightly together as possible and go straight into the house when we got back.

When we finally arrived home, I had to get out before the boy and do this kind of weird pigeon walk, tucking my butt under because I was convinced that was the only way he wouldn't see. I don't know whether it worked. At last, I reached the safety of my room, but that was still only halfway—because then there was the cleanup. Were my fabulous white overalls ever going to be white again? I tried desperately to determine whether hot water or cold water was going to get this stain out, filling a big bowl with every type of cleaning product I could find (for future reference, always use COLD WATER!). Then I hid my sorry-looking overalls in the laundry basket and hoped for the best. But they were never the same again. They would forever be as stained as my memory of that day AND my confidence in my

period calendar! Suddenly this so-called "curse of womanhood" all made sense and it made me feel depressed. . . .

Anyway, I am so grateful now for my period app. I can track my different phases and understand why I might be having belly pain or breakouts or more discharge. Though even with the app, I know not to be surprised if my period is a day or two early or late and that things like stress and travel can cause it to break its regular pattern altogether and just show up. Which is what happened to me AGAIN the other day when I was wearing—wait for it—white jeans! I went to get lunch and just as I got to the restaurant I realized I had started bleeding. I felt confident that I wasn't going to bleed THROUGH because I am, of course, much older now and know my body so much better, so I picked up my lunch and walked back to this theater where I was performing that night. But when I got to the bathroom I was in exactly the same state as I had been twenty years ago. The only difference was that this time I was far less embarrassed. And luckily, I had a change of clothes!

INHALE

EXHALE

24

GENERATION OLD

• • • • •

I was around thirteen when my parents started irritating me. Literally every single thing they said was annoying. It took a few years till that went away, and now my mom is my #1! I am always so excited to talk to her and tell her what I've been doing—she is always there to listen to me and I appreciate it so much. Being a mom must be so intense—I don't know how she did it; I am amazed when I think about it. Giving up all your time to look after someone else . . . I am forever grateful! But for a while there I thought she was desperately uncool and I was not interested in ANYTHING she had to say. Parents (or whoever looks after you) sticking their noses in when you don't want them around is the worst. . . . Embarrassing you in front of your friends, having NO IDEA what good music sounds like, or not understanding why a certain pair of sneakers is 50,000 times better than an off-brand, cheaper pair.

But the thing is, they have gone through all of this themselves! They were young once; they went through school and sweaty years and will have great tips and ideas from their own experiences. Letting them pass these on to you could even make for some good bonding. My mom was my biggest source of information for all things body-related and I would ask her EVERYTHING. She always had a story about something that had happened to her that was similar to whatever I was feeling. The fact is, clothes, music, and technology might change, but people's experiences stay pretty much the same.

At the end of the day, even when I was embarrassed of her, I knew deep down that she was the best. She brought me into this world and gave me the opportunity to LIVE! That's something that can never be changed and I've always felt pretty grateful. So—give generation old a chance. I promise you, they're doing their best!

THERE IS NO
LIKE THAT
TWO WOMEN
CHOSEN TO

INTIMACY
BETWEEN
WHO HAVE
BE SISTERS.

— Warsan Shire

25

VIRTUAL REALITY

• • • • •

Makeup is super fun. I love it as much as the next show girl and it's such a great way to experiment with different looks, themes, styles, and how you're feeling on a certain day. But when it becomes a mask that you can't leave the house without, you need to pause and think about why you are using it. Are you trying to disguise the way you really look? Are you aspiring to the impossible? Because, the fact is, filters and Photoshop are everywhere. You can't trust anything you see! That perfect bikini body? That flawless face? Everything online or in print is retouched. There is no point comparing yourself with what you see in magazines—E-V-E-RY-THING has been altered in some way—like teeth being made whiter and skin made tighter. Women have been looking at magazines and billboards for years, comparing themselves to figures they believe to

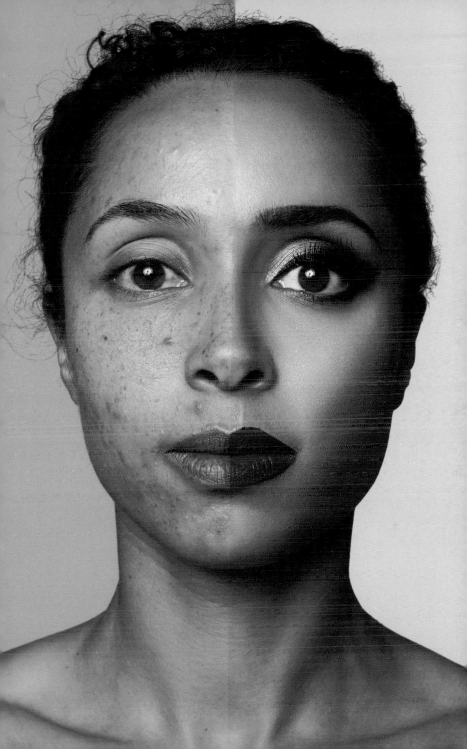

be "ideal" or examples of "perfection" that are not even REAL PEOPLE! Don't compare yourself to magazines. In fact, cross "comparing" off your list altogether! Comparing yourself to anyone is a surefire way to make you feel bad. We are all different, and there are beautiful and lovable things about all of us that a retouched image can never hope to express. Whatever your face, whatever your shape, embrace it, love it, cover it in moisturizer, stretch it out, and don't lose touch with it. Society and the media have taken it so far that we are now finding ways to recreate Photoshop in real life—using products on our skin with names like Photo Finish! It's so crazy, right?! Rise above all the trashy magazines and know that a girl who likes herself, looks good. Period.

26

FEED YOUR BRAIN

• • • • •

Your brain is like a muscle and, like all muscles, it needs stimulation to stay fit. You need to keep feeding and exercising it! And you really need to think about WHAT you are feeding it. You wouldn't eat chocolate bars for every meal and expect your body to work at its full potential—in the same way you don't want to feed your brain uninspiring trash!

The internet is an amazing source of stimulation, but the way we use it can get really stale. You end up looking at the same videos, hearing the same songs, playing the same games . . . Switching things up will exercise your brain and lead you to new places. Every so often, check out new websites (with your parents' permission). Look up a question you might have; search for events or people you're interested in; or find blogs for hobbies you'd like to try. There's a whole world out there, but we often stick to the same little parts we know. I like to make myself listen to music I wouldn't normally listen to—even if I hate it! I try to listen to the whole song to see how it makes me feel by the end and what sorts of images it creates in my mind. Sometimes I reimagine music videos for songs I like—music is a great way to let your imagination go somewhere new.

And while in one sense the internet can take you anywhere without you even leaving your house, the truth is you are just sitting, looking at a screen. It's hard to stay away from technology—for adults, too—but getting out into the real world and seeing and doing things is a completely different experience from hunching over a phone or laptop. Be open to new things, even if you think they might be boring. Learn a card trick, pick up a book you wouldn't usually read, or make a model airplane! Keep exploring wherever you go—fill your brain with the best quality ideas, challenges, images, sounds, and colors!

NOTHING WILL WORK

● start

end

UNLESS YOU DO

— Maya Angelou

27

IF ONLY . . .

• • • • •

"If only" is that tiny voice in your head telling you that if only you had a smaller nose/shinier hair/longer legs, then everything would be okay.

Everyone experiences wanting what they don't have at some point in life. But when it's about your body, it can feel harder; it can be tied up with how much you value yourself and think other people value you. "If only" is TOXIC. It means you're never satisfied. The fact is, your legs probably aren't going to get longer, BUT you have tons of other amazing things about you. And—trust me—liking yourself and your own shape is the most attractive quality anyone can have. Sometimes when I was younger, I would catch myself thinking that if only I'd been born in the 1950s, or lived in a different country, my body shape would have been more "right." But eventually I realized the most appealing

thing about another person is when they are comfortable in their own skin. Sooooo much easier said than done but it's really true.

It also seems silly to want to be a particular way when there are so many different ideas of beauty right now all over the world. I travel a lot, and I find it absurd that in countries where most women have dark skin, the supermarket shelves are filled with dangerous bleaching creams to make complexions lighter—while women in other parts of the world with white skin risk skin cancer by baking themselves at tanning salons or the beach in pursuit of a "healthy" tan.

So stop giving yourself such a hard time and take a look at yourself. What's nice about you? What DO you like? What would you never change? Congratulate yourself on these things! Write them down if you want. Then, when you feel the "if only"s coming back, read them again and remind yourself that you have a lot of qualities that are GREAT! Give yourself a high five in the mirror and smile!

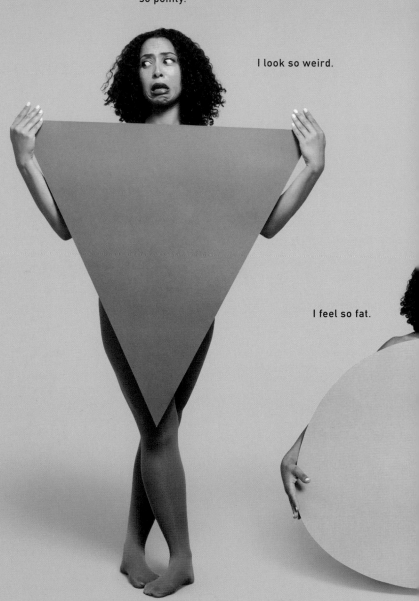

Yes, look at my great shape!

I love my tummy.

So sharp!

Loving my angles.

I'm a curvy crusader!

28

STRETCH MARKS

• • • • •

Stretch marks can happen and, if they do, there is no way around 'em. They are annoying but they also fade. They come up in places where you are E-X-P-A-N-D-I-N-G and the skin has to stretch quickly to accommodate your new body. I got them on my legs, my butt, and all over my new boobs. They can be pretty scary at first and can be anything from skin-colored to pink or purple. I was so upset when they appeared all over my boobs like spider webs—I thought I would never be able to wear a scoop-neck shirt again. But eventually I did! You just have to get over it and own them. Some girls really celebrate their stretch marks now, which is GREAT—you can't avoid them so you might as well embrace them!

> FACT: If you lather yourself in moisturizer every day you can reduce stretch marks. But just know that most will fade over time.

HAIR TODAY, GONE TOMORROW

• • • • •

If you decide there are parts of your body you want hair free, here's the lowdown:

 Trimming

This is removing the hair from where it grows out of the skin. Because you are snipping it halfway up (each hair has a root beneath the skin, like a plant!), the hair can grow back looking thicker. But it's the cheapest and easiest DIY route.

SHAVING: watch the sharp blades; please don't cut yourself! Also make sure you do it with wet legs—the first time I did it was with dry legs and it was so itchy. Afterward, moisturize your skin.

HAIR REMOVAL CREAMS: buy at a drugstore, put some on the hair, and . . . melt it away. It's quick and easy, though I don't like to think about what those chemicals are doing to your skin.

| PROS: quick, cheap, with total smoothness at first. |
| CONS: possible rash and scratchy regrowth stubble after a day or two. |

Plucking

Yes, like a chicken. I mean pulling the hair out by its root (ouch!) so that when it grows back it's soft, not stubbly. You do have to make sure it's long enough before you can do it again, though—which can be annoying if the party is on Saturday but the hair is so short that it won't be ready to pluck out before Tuesday. . . .

 WAXING: expensive at the salon, messy at home. Wax strips are easiest, but be careful not to let them touch anything other than you —it's impossible to get the wax off. Press one on, then whip it off fast, like a giant Band-Aid— yeeouch!

 THREADING: a beautician runs twisted thread along the skin, plucking out any hair along the way. It's not one to try without a professional, but there are lots of threading salons everywhere,

 DEPILATORY: a little machine you can buy that has whirring discs that spin next to one another, catching your hairs as you pass it over them and whipping 'em out. These machines don't cost much more than a wax at the salon but they last for years.

PROS: lasts for weeks with soft regrowth.
CONS: hurts a little; costs a little more; sometimes the hairs get stuck under your skin when they're growing back and cause spots and in-grown hairs.

30

I ♥ THE WORD FAT!

• • • • •

Fat gets a bad rep in the press. But you HAVE to have some, even if it's just a bit—it's essential for living! Some of us have those jelly genes that make us put on extra weight as we get womanly curves—it's completely normal. In general, getting chubby didn't bother me too much—I felt like I ate really well and did a lot of exercise, so at first I was confused when I started putting on weight. I thought maybe I was doing something wrong. But you can be totally healthy and have some wobble and jelly on you, too! You are getting taller and growing boobs 'n' things, so extra weight elsewhere is going to happen. It can feel heavy, and if it happens quickly, your clothes can suddenly feel tight. But don't worry—it means you're becoming a woman. So embrace thy thighs! Fat is fun! It keeps you warm! Plus, every seat is comfortable. Figure out what to wear to make yourself feel good and over time your curves will feel more familiar. Don't panic if it feels like a shock at first—it is a really big thing to get used to a new body shape!

That said, don't let putting on weight hold you down—literally. You want to resist falling into the "I'm sooo bored and tired; I've got my period; leave me alone I will eat this whole package of chocolate chip cookies if I want to" mode—that will probably just leave you feeling bad about yourself. Sure, every now and then we need to chill, but you also need to be getting a good amount of exercise. Build those muscles! Exercise may start to feel like your enemy—when I put on weight, I suddenly hated running—but I still enjoyed trampolining and roller-skating. You have to do what feels right for you, whether it's tennis, yoga, soccer, t'ai chi—whatever. Instead of trying to control and suppress your new body, see how you can work with it. Try to focus on what you can do to help your body and make it grow STRONG.

31

DO NOT BECOME A STRANGER TO YOURSELF BY BLENDING IN WITH

144

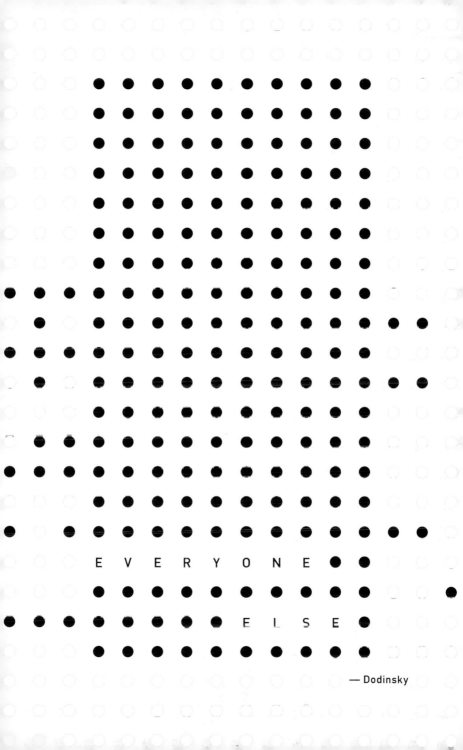

EVERYONE ELSE

— Dodinsky

32

CH—CH—CH—

• • • • •

Something happened to me the summer I was twelve. My body was filling out and getting rounder and suddenly, one day, every step caused my inner thighs to rub together! Before I had even made it ten feet out of the house, I had an irritated hot red patch of chafed thigh at the top of my legs. OUCH!

To keep it from happening again, I wore cotton bike shorts under my school uniform every day. This probably didn't help when I

CH—CHAFING!

had a yeast infection (see page 198)—since they were tight and no doubt made me sweatier—but it definitely helped my legs glide past each other without rubbing. Sweaty summer legs are the quickest way to end up with a whole lot of chafe. If it's a hot day and your legs tend to rub together, try to remember that when you're getting dressed in the morning so you can save yourself from pain later!

33

BUTTS

• • • • •

I love my butt—always have. When I was young, it was bigger and big butts were not fashionable. In those days, the waif look was in—pretty much just skin and bone. But I still loved my butt! It was like a personal cushion and a very useful muscle for running and dancing. The only thing that has ever annoyed me about it is that NO PANTS FIT. EVER. If I could get my legs into them, then there would be a huge gap at the waist, or if the waist fit then they would be so tight around my thighs that I couldn't move. The only ones that ever fit all over were a vintage pair from the 1950s that I found at a secondhand store. These pants seemed to understand the curves of a woman— because that was the shape that was fashion-able then. They were tailored to go out at the thigh and hip and then come back in at the waist. Now I look at skinny jeans and know there is NO

WAY my arm—let alone my leg!—is going to fit. It seems so unfair that all these pants are allegedly designed for the latest shape, when most of the population looks nothing like that! Millions of women try to cram themselves into a fabric cage and then feel bad because their beautiful bodies don't fit.

And don't talk to me about underwear—sheesh . . . For years I had a permanent wedgie! I would put them on, take three steps, and they would be up my behind. I tried everything: boy leg, bikini, low rise, fuller cut . . . I would have to go to the bathroom just to unwedge myself, pull my undies down as low as possible, and hope that they would stay there until I was at least back in class—it was so uncomfortable! Finally, I made my own: my friend worked in fashion and we made a pair of wedge-proof underwear. I spent weeks testing them out until we found the perfect design that would stay PUT!

So I say LOVE your butt, look after it, and dress it so that it looks its best, regardless of fashion!

34

HOTHOTHOT

• • • • •

Sometimes it feels like sexy images are everywhere. Over the last hundred years, sex has gone from being a subject no one talked about to the #1 way of advertising everything from deodorant to spaghetti. It's in music videos, on billboards, all over magazines—and it's confusing! Before you even start exploring for yourself, you'll have been bombarded with images suggesting sexy things. Weird, right?! The important thing to remember is that much of what we see via advertising and music videos are not real-life scenarios or even real-life people.

So, what's a girl to do?

Well, while it's very normal to feel interested in sex, my advice is to wait until you're older. There's no perfect time to lose your virginity and no rules about who, how, what, where, and when. Your virginity—like your body—is YOURS and only YOU get to decide what you do with it. For instance, I remember being ten or eleven when I REALLY learned what "butterflies in your tummy" meant! It was this weird sensation I got when I saw someone I had a crush on. I never told anyone, even my best friend, that I had a crush—I was so embarrassed!! But every time I saw them, or even just thought about them, I felt a wave come over me: all hot and tingly, kind of funny in my tummy. It's when you can't stop thinking about someone and little things remind you of them—which makes you think about them and then you get hot and sweaty and it's weeeeird!! I clearly had it bad . . . but did I want to *be with them* in that way, the way I saw on TV and in movies?

I felt like, NO WAY! But I also wasn't sure. . . . It was a whole new set of feelings I was still getting used to. Later I realized ALL OF THIS has to do with the hormones that kick in during puberty. During this time, so many things are going on in our bodies all at once!! You're going to be confused about sex and feelings and attraction and crushes—but take your time, don't stress, and above all, remember it's all NORMAL.

153

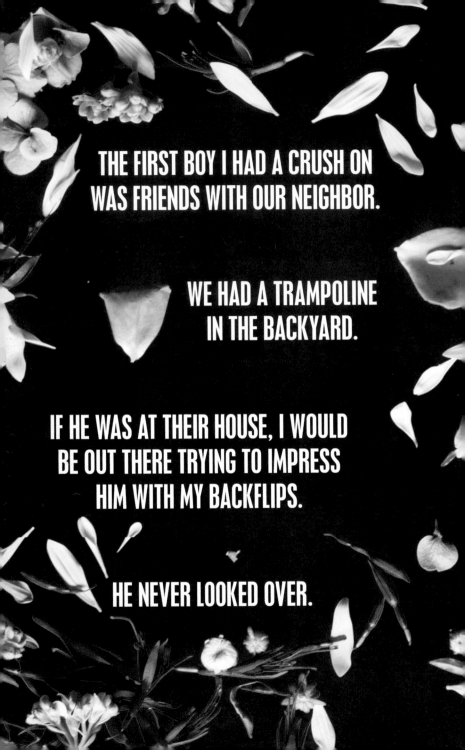

THE FIRST BOY I HAD A CRUSH ON
WAS FRIENDS WITH OUR NEIGHBOR.

WE HAD A TRAMPOLINE
IN THE BACKYARD.

IF HE WAS AT THEIR HOUSE, I WOULD
BE OUT THERE TRYING TO IMPRESS
HIM WITH MY BACKFLIPS.

HE NEVER LOOKED OVER.

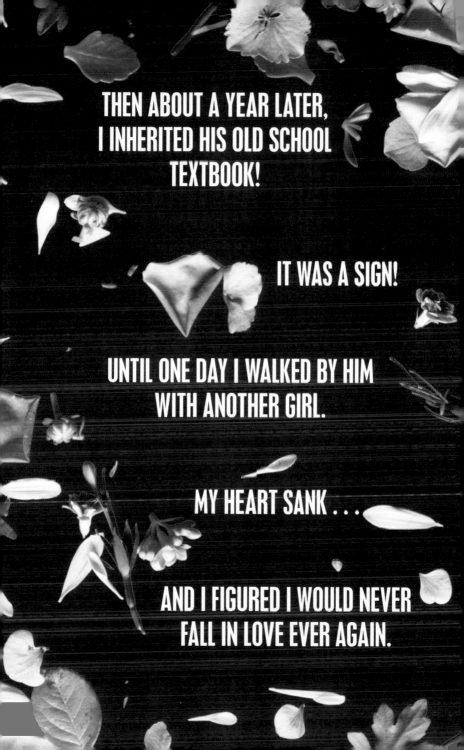

THEN ABOUT A YEAR LATER,
I INHERITED HIS OLD SCHOOL
TEXTBOOK!

IT WAS A SIGN!

UNTIL ONE DAY I WALKED BY HIM
WITH ANOTHER GIRL.

MY HEART SANK . . .

AND I FIGURED I WOULD NEVER
FALL IN LOVE EVER AGAIN.

35

TIDAL MOODS AND HOR-MOANS

• • • • •

I am really into the moon—any time I start feeling not myself, I check the calendar and it's usually around full-moon time. The moon has a huge effect on the oceans. It controls the tides, and since our bodies are made up of 65 percent water, it makes sense that we have our own tides, too, sometimes high and sometimes low. It's really not just an old wives' tale!

Anyway, emotions get heightened when hormones start hanging out at PU-BER-TY. I could go from normal Marawa to stone-faced DO NOT TALK TO ME OR I WILL PUNCH YOU SO HARD YOU WON'T WAKE UP TILL CHRISTMAS Marawa in a nanosecond, just because someone had looked at me funny. And sometimes, when my mom asked me for the tenth time, "What

I love
everybody!

BLURGH

is wrong? Do you want a cup of tea?" I would storm off to my room, screaming, and then when I got there, not be entirely sure what was even wrong. But I would stick to my mood for at least an hour or two—just to be consistent.

Meanwhile, your friends are all doing it, too! One minute they're cool, the next they're whispering around you and giving you blank looks, then they're your best friends again. Ugh. It's really a full-time job keeping up with all of this—let alone getting homework done.

So what's my advice? Be kind. Your feelings are real, of course! But maybe you don't need to take them out on everyone else. Looking back, I could have said, "I'm just feeling a bit off today, Mom, I don't know why. And NO—thank you— NO tea."

Sometimes when I'm in that zone I can tell it's happening, and I try really hard not to take it out on others. The best thing about this is you become aware that maybe your friend who's being weird is just having an off day, too!

36

ASKING FOR ASPIRIN

· · · · ·

There are lots of different types of pain. Some pains are just the daily aches of being a human. Like growing pains—my knees used to hurt so much, my mom would give me two hot water bottles to wrap around them. And period pain—at school, girls would always ask to go to the nurse for some aspirin at the first sign. No one wants to be in pain—why would they? Which is why it's easy to start relying on painkillers, but over time, it's not great to be constantly putting them into your body. Stretching can be a great alternative to help relieve headaches, period pain, stomach, and muscle pain. Try some of the stretches on the following pages before you reach for the pills. . . .

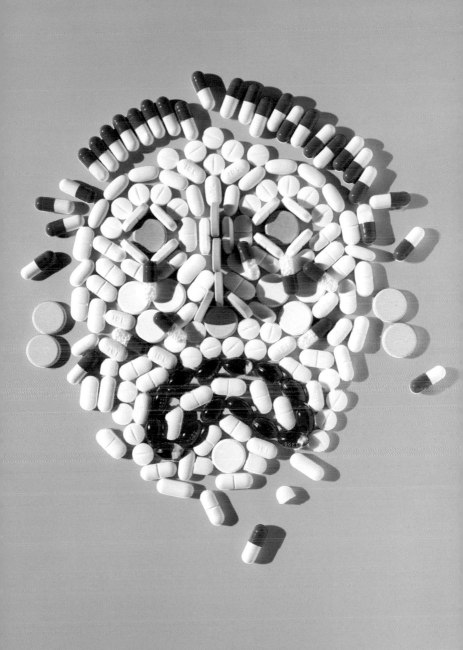

37

STRE-E-E-E-ETCH

● ● ● ● ●

Stretching makes you feel gooood. It sends fresh blood flowing into your muscles, warming them up and helping them relax. It relieves tension in your body, like period pain or a sore neck and—over time—it improves your flexibility. One thing: It's important not to overstretch and push harder when it already hurts. Be patient—find a stretch that feels only a little uncomfortable and then focus on your breathing, taking long, deep breaths in and out and staying in the stretch as long as you can (sixty seconds is ideal). In fact, practicing deep breathing is key! You can really relax and calm your mind and body through deep, regular breaths—try it!

KNOTTY NECK

Stand with your back against a wall and then gently sink your head forward until you've got a really good double chin. Take a deep breath and come back out. Then gently tilt your head to one side, so you feel a stretch across the opposite side of your neck. Take a deep breath and come back to the center. Repeat on the other side. Never roll your neck around in full circles—always come back to looking straight ahead between each stretch.

TIGHT SHOULDERS

If you're on the computer too much or even texting a lot, sometimes your shoulders can get really tight. To release some tension, bring your shoulders right up to your ears—squeeze them up! Then drop and relax them. Repeat five or six times! You can also swing your arms around your body and shake it out, shake it out! This will help loosen up your shoulders.

NO-FUN KNEES

Those growing pains in my knees—yeeouch! Stretch your calves by standing on a step and letting your heels drop down low, or try doing little knee circles with your hands on your knees and your feet together. Resting an ankle on the opposite knee and letting your knee fall out to the side also feels good. Even just lying down with your feet raised on a cushion can help the blood flow.

BAD BACK

With bent knees and feet together, try bending over to touch your toes—this is a really good one to stretch out your lower back. From here you can also walk in place to really feel it in each hip and on each side. Then—I love this—lie on your back, bring your knees up to your chest, and hug them. Then rock from side-to-side. Great for period pain.

CHURNING STOMACH

Lie on your back with your palms facing up, your legs relaxed, and toes falling outward. Breathe deeply and imagine you are breathing into your belly button—making it push out. Don't use your muscles to push out, though, let the air do it! Once you are breathing deeply, count 10 breaths or 20 if you have time! This will really help you relax.

HUNCHY HANDS

Start by stretching all your fingers out as far as you can— and holding that for 10–20 seconds. Put all your fingers together and point them down toward your wrist, to stretch out the back of your hand. Then, put your hands together in a prayer position and bring your elbows up, keeping your wrists together to stretch the front of your wrist.

PERIOD PAINS

Child's pose is my favorite period pain-relief pose: You kneel on the floor, sitting on your ankles, and then stretch your arms up high as you breathe in. Then, exhale and stretch your arms out far in front, with your forehead on the ground. You can stay here for ages—don't fall asleep! It is really relaxing and helps to relieve stomach cramps.

HIP, HIP, HOORAY!

This is amazing for stretching out your legs and also taking pressure off your lower back. Make sure your knee is on something soft. Then, think about tucking your hips under so that you get a great stretch along the front of your leg and hip. Try to stay there for three deep breaths. Then, straighten your front leg and stretch your hamstring out, too!

38

MEDITAAAAAATION

• • • • •

Phones, computers, school, friends, family . . . everything! Sometimes it all gets to be a bit much and your head feels kind of full. Sometimes you just need to take ten to twenty minutes to reset. And the good news is that you can! Anywhere! At home, in your room, in the bathroom—wherever! Here is how I like to take a li'l break:

Turn everything off—phone, laptop, music . . . even the lights if you want. You can lie, sit, have your eyes open or closed. Whatever works for you—this is YOUR time.

Now. Think about your breathing and nothing else. Try to make your mind like a clear, blue sky. Thoughts will come, but try to let them pass through your mind like clouds that you watch until they are gone, leaving your mind clear and blue again. Listen to your breath going in and out. Try to breathe as deeply as possible, letting

your tummy relax and expand with each breath. If you feel your mind wandering off, thinking about something you wish you hadn't said or how your red sweater would look really good with your new jeans, just gently remind yourself that this is your time for a clear mind and try to bring your focus back to your breath. As you breathe out, you can visualize that thought as a cloud you're pushing away to keep your mind's sky clear and blue.

HELPFUL HINTS

Set an alarm

If you find that you get nervous about falling asleep or losing track of time, set an alarm! Setting yourself a goal of meditating ten minutes every day with an alarm is also a really good way to get your body into the practice of meditation—even if for the first few days your brain is firing with tons of thoughts. Gradually, you'll train your mind to recognize switch-off time and it will become calmer more quickly.

Don't stress about stress!

Don't get frustrated with yourself if you can't switch off your mind. When I'm really stressed I can never get it to stop! One thing I find useful is to have a pen and paper handy and write down everything I'm thinking

about—every worry, fear, and thought. Once I have
written it down, my mind feels ready to relax and
let go of all the things I wrote. Then I can
sit with a clear mind.

Breathe

Everything always comes back to breath—everything
starts here. Make sure you are breathing deep breaths
and letting the tension in your belly fade away.

Get comfy!

Ideally you want to be sitting or lying in a comfortable
position—I always get cold when I sit still, so I make
sure I have an extra sweater or blanket wrapped
around me before I start. Everyone has a different
favorite position—see what works best for you!

Find the quiet

You don't want to be trying to meditate in the same
room as someone who is practicing how to play a
trumpet or chopping up onions—try to find a quiet
place where you are unlikely to be bothered.

Aftereffects

Sometimes after meditating you can be a bit slow to
jump back into reality, so make sure you take a second
to stand up slowly, check how you feel, and take a deep
breath. You may also get hit with inspiration for how to
solve a problem or something you want to remember,
so that pen and paper will be put to good use.

39

SLEEP

· · · · ·

Apart from food and water, sleep is THE MOST IMPORTANT THING! And that means restful sleep—the kind where you dream about jumping in slow motion across pastel clouds while a brass band plays your favorite song. . . . Going to sleep and waking up at the same time each day is key! It really helps your body clock stay regular. When you don't get enough sleep, everything can seem a bit off the next day and more difficult or annoying. If you can't sleep because you're worrying or thinking about stuff, it can help to write it down! Same thing as when you're meditating. Keep a pen and paper next to your bed—once you get your worries out of your head and on to paper then your mind is clear to float off to la-la land! You could also try stretching (see page 164), meditating (see page 170), or lavender spray (try a health-food store.)

& WORKS REALLY HARD even while you SLEEP.

Please Learn to LOVE HER.

~YOUR BODY

— Loren

40

UNHAPPY EATING

• • • • •

Your diet just means the food and drink you put into your body. Your body needs fuel to work—at least three healthy meals a day, as well as snacks, if you're active and growing. Some people go on "diets," which usually means they reduce the amount of fuel their bodies take in so they lose weight. But if you are not overweight to begin with, it's dangerous to cut back on your body's fuel. Your energy runs low, your mind can have trouble focusing, and your moods change. When I was in high school, I never dieted but I had friends who did on and off. I thought it was kinda weird and pretty boring—the moment someone goes on a diet it seems like all they can think or talk about is food. . . . Anyway, one friend started dieting but something about it was different. She started getting thinner and thinner—everyone was worried about her and tried to get her to eat, but she would say, "Oh, I just ate lunch," or find some other excuse. Eventually she had to leave school and was in the hospital for a while. She was anorexic and had nearly starved herself to death. It took her a long time to recover, but she has managed to get on top of her eating disorder and get healthy!

People develop eating disorders for all kinds of reasons, but often as a result of something difficult that happened to them in the past. If they don't feel in control, they may feel that controlling what they eat gives them back power (even though this is not logical). Once you get to a certain point with dieting, your brain starts thinking differently. If you think that you or a friend are beginning to obsess about food or aren't eating enough, then there's lots of help out there. Talk to a close adult and do some research—there will be plenty of advice from federal and state organizations (don't bother with message boards—you'll never get the facts there). It's perfectly possible to sort out, and the sooner you do, the better.

41

GIRLS FOR GIRLS

· · · · ·

Pick up any gossip magazine and read the comments made about women. It's as though the only important things for us to worry about are other women's waistlines and whether they're wearing the right clothes. This culture of women putting other women down is an easy habit to fall into, but I think it's really sad. It makes people insecure and pits women against one another. It's important to see how destructive this is— competitiveness is for the racetrack, not the street of sisterhood. It's crazy to work against each other. We need to support each other; be a team! The word FEMINISM means different things to different people. For me, it's pretty simple and I couldn't put it better than the great author Maya Angelou: "I'm a feminist. I've been a female for a long time now. It'd be stupid not to be on my own side."

TEAM

MAKE

DREAM

WORK THE WORK*

*It's not just a catchy phrase
—it's the truth.

42

THAT WAS WEIRD

· · · · ·

As I mentioned in the first chapter, when I got older and my body started to change shape, people began looking at me differently. One thing that bugged me a lot was the way men I didn't know—total strangers—would look at me in this creepy way. For whatever reason, some men think it's okay not to talk or look at you like you're a human being, instead behaving as if you're something to be looked at or commented on—as if you're an exhibit in a show! It made me feel uncomfortable, like I had done something wrong without knowing it.

One time, when I was really young—maybe eight?—I was in the supermarket and a guy passed by me and squeezed my butt. URGH, it was so gross! I glared at him. It had happened so fast and I was shocked at how he ignored me and walked off like nothing had happened.

186

I was with my mom (who hadn't seen), but I didn't know what to say, so I said nothing. I was embarrassed! Later, I began to understand the importance of speaking up. For nearly twenty years I have played that moment over in my mind, thinking of different versions where I kick him or karate chop him in the face! Now I feel a lot more confident about saying something or asking for help if something like this happens, but it can be really hard to do. You just want the moment to go away as quickly as possible— and making a scene seems like it's going to prolong the icky feeling you have or make people wonder what *you* did wrong.

But if you feel safe to act on it there and then, you've got to try to do it! It's important to be strong and expose this kind of behavior. You also need to judge the situation. And if you don't feel safe to act on it in the moment, please do tell someone you trust as soon as you can after. It'll make you feel better, I promise.

THE POOP STORY

• • • • •

Once, I was at school and the part of the building I was in only had one toilet. I was on my way to the bathroom during class because I had to do a massive #2. I always get panicked about #2 because I want it to happen with no one knowing it happened—I always want to disguise it as a #1. I quickly flush so it doesn't smell so much, spray a little

air freshener if there is some (a big spray will smell so strongly that everyone will know anyway), and—most important—make sure it goes down.

So, I ran to the bathroom as quickly as I could, so it wouldn't seem like I had been gone longer than a normal pee trip, and then got on with business. I did a perfect poop. One text-book example, straight, intact poop. Happy that this was all happening in good time and I could make it back to class without anyone knowing what I had done, I flushed and stood watching, ready to wave good-bye to perfection. . . .

Nothing happened. NO SUCK! No flush! No good-bye! The toilet just filled with water a bit. My heart started to speed up. Okay, extra water might help it go faster . . . I flushed again and held the handle down. My poop floated higher and higher as more water flooded the bowl. Horrified, I let go but the water kept coming until, finally, I was looking at a full bowl of water with a perfect poop slowly bobbing from one side to the other, smiling up at me.

OMG.

Remember: one toilet. Whoever went next was going to know it was me. I couldn't risk flushing one more time—it would overflow for sure. The only option was removal.

I looked around the bathroom at my options. Air freshener—spray it till it dissolves? Push it down the toilet bowl with my bare hands? With a toilet paper roll? Scoop it up?

ARGHHHH!!!

Plastic—there was a plastic liner in the trash can. Okay, this could work. I got the plastic bag. BUT THEN WHAT? Put it in the bag AND

THEN WHAT??? I couldn't put it back in the trash. I couldn't take it back to class . . . The sanitary bin. The sanitary bin with its one-way lid. This was it! Scoop the poop, tie the bag so it didn't smell, and put it in the sanitary bin. I had to put my hands in the toilet. Both of them—protected by a thin layer of plastic bag. I scooped and gagged. I tied. I won. The toilet was full of water but that was the next person's problem—there was no evidence of *my* special package. I washed my hands about twenty times and gave a li'l victory squirt of air freshener . . . and ran back to class.

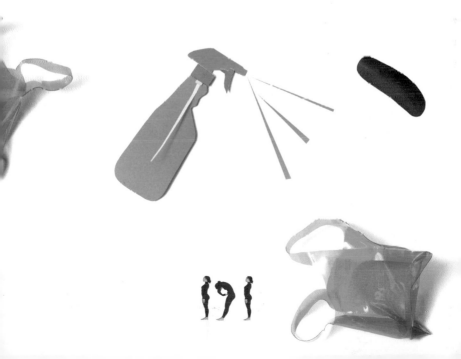

44

YOUR GENDER, YOUR CHOICE

· · · · ·

As kids, both my brothers LOVED wearing dresses—way more than I did. It was never a big deal in my family; no one was judged for dressing a particular way. Unfortunately, not everyone has such an easy time growing up and exploring their identity.

We are all made uniquely in terms of how we look and feel. And as long as it's not hurting anyone else, there is no reason someone should be judged for how they dress or express themselves. I say wear the clothes you want, do the things you want, and above all, love the people you want! Nearly every movie, TV show, and book you come across as you are growing up will probably have some kind of love interest— and almost always it will be a boy who likes a girl or a girl who likes a boy. But, in real life, that's just not how it is for everyone. Some boys like boys. Some girls like girls. Some boys feel they ARE girls and were born in the wrong bodies. Some girls feel they are boys in the wrong bodies. It's complicated!

But there is no wrong gender for any person, and judging people or treating them differently because of their gender isn't okay—we are all human at the end of the day. Not allowing someone, especially friends, to express their identity is not nice or helpful, particularly if they're having a hard time working out how they feel about themselves. Girls, boys, or people who don't identify as a girl or a boy are all equal.

These days there is far more freedom to be who you are than there was in the past. Don't stress. There's plenty of time! No matter what your friends tell you, or your parents want from you—or you want from yourself—eventually you'll figure out who you really are.

45

FASHION vs. STYLE

• • • • •

Okay, so, fashion and style are two VERY different things, and as soon as you understand the difference between them, you'll feel much freer. Fashion is basically what you see in store windows or on every second girl at the mall—and it will change regularly. Things that were the IT items last week are suddenly half price and very uncool. Style is more timeless and is about wearing clothes that suit you and that you love!

Fast fashion can be fun, but it moves on swiftly. It's a quick fix and if all you do is fashion, it can be really expensive and annoying because you have to continue buying things to keep up, knowing that in a few weeks or months you wouldn't want to be caught dead in that outfit. The trick is to mix pieces of fashion with your own style until you find your groove. Style can last a lifetime and also change with your mood.

You can find inspiration for your style everywhere—old photographs, magazines, blogs, online, vintage shops, and flea markets can all provide inspiration for new looks you might want to try in the safety of your bedroom, before unleashing them on the world. Some people find a look they like and stick with it forever. Others experiment and try out tons of different looks, hairstyles, and accessories. Sometimes it's nice to feel part of a crew with your friends by wearing the same style. This can often be linked to the type of music you listen to or other things you find inspiring at the time. Your style, like your bra size, will probably change a lot over the years. Personally, I have been through many phases: Bantu, almost goth, raver, hip-hop. Embrace trying new things! The great thing about personal style is that when you find things you LOVE to wear, you feel comfortable and confident and this in turn makes you look great! Confidence can often be found in your favorite outfit. Go for it—you only live once!

46
YEAST

· · · · ·

A yeast infection starts when tiny yeasty fungi, called candida, that live in your vagina, multiply. This leads to a bunch of really irritating symptoms!

So why do candida start multiplying? Good question. Stress; tight clothes; changes in your diet; changes in your hormones around the time you get your period; using tampons at the end of your period when your vagina is too dry . . . all these things can trigger overproduction of yeast, leading to an infection.

For most people, the symptoms of a yeast infection are one or any of the following: itchiness; a white, lumpy discharge like cottage cheese; and sometimes redness and swelling around the vagina. None of these things will make you feel like the cutest girl in town, but just remember: it is not a permanent thing and is

really easy to cure. Yeast infections affect pretty much all women at some point. For some it's a one-off, for others it's a recurring drama like it is for me. I had yeast infections on and off for years and it drove me CRAZY. I tried everything and I just couldn't get rid of it. It made me feel gross, hot, and bothered. But now I have a wealth of wonderful yeast-busting tips to pass on to you!

DON'T worry! Yeast infections are REALLY common and affect most people at some point. However . . .

DO go to the doctor if you haven't had one before, just to make sure you have the right diagnosis.

DON'T wear shiny, synthetic undies or tights. They won't let your skin breathe, instead creating a little heat trap down there for growing bacteria.

DO wear clean, comfy cotton underwear to let your sensitive skin breathe! You can also get special pure-silk ones, which are great for people with eczema.

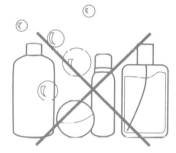

DON'T use douches, perfumed soaps, vaginal deodorants (don't use these anyway!), or wipes, as these will just irritate the skin even further.

DO keep your vagina clean. Rinse it lots and wash front to back with clean water once a day.

DON'T think that sitting in a bowl of yogurt will cure it. But it might help with the symptoms and feel lovely and cool.

DO go to the doctor, who will prescribe you medication and a cream.

47

PEE—OUCH!

● ● ● ● ●

Once, when I was little, I was running around in a field naked and I managed to get a tiny piece of hay or something stuck right up my pee hole. I didn't realize what had happened until I needed to go to the bathroom and felt a sudden, searing pain. I spent two days refusing to go to the bathroom until my mom took me to the doctor, who managed to get the piece of hay out. Then, when I was older and got an infection up my pee hole (a urinary tract infection, or UTI), the burning feeling felt familiar!

UTIs are caused by bacteria getting into your pee hole. It's the main reason why we are taught to wipe front to back. Other things can bring them on, too—dehydration, tight jeans, underwear that isn't made of cotton. I don't mean to put you off those last two, but just so you know! When you have a UTI, you feel like you need to pee all the time, but when you do it feels like intense burning. Sometimes you also see blood in your urine, so basically the last thing you want to do is pee, but that's one of the most important things to do! You need to drink lots of water to help flush out the infection. If it's bad, you may also need to go to the doctor for antibiotics. ☹

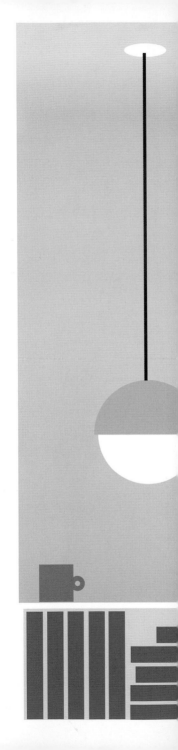

48

STAYING IN CONTROL

• • • • •

This one is simple: JUST SAY NO. That might be a really boring response, but I am pretty boring when it comes to drug advice. I was never interested. I wanted to be in control of my body.

It's hard if you find yourself in a situation where people around you are drinking alcohol or (even) taking drugs—but that doesn't mean YOU have to do those things. Alcohol and drugs can cause real problems with your mental

and physical health so, if you want to take care of yourself, don't let anyone pressure you into doing anything you don't want to do. Easy to say, harder to practice! But if someone is going to judge you and make you feel bad about your decisions, then that's their problem and it means they're not a good friend anyway. A true friend is someone who you can share a big stack of blueberry pancakes with and they let you have the last bite! A true friend is someone who loves you for who you are—not who they want you to be.

49

LAST, BUT NOT LEAST

· · · · ·

There's so much more I want to tell you! But I have officially run out of room! So here are all the little tidbits I couldn't get in elsewhere:

Write a letter to your future self—you could write to your sixteen-year-old self or twenty-one-year-old self. It's always fun to write what you think you will be doing when you are that age—and even weirder to open it up years later and see how much has changed!

———

Make my energy ball recipe: Dates, shredded coconut, cacao powder, and cranberries. Mix them all in a food processor, then squish into balls and roll in more coconut—so easy! So tasty! And FULL of energy. Make them on Sunday and enjoy them all week.

———

Look up Misty Copeland, a solo ballerina with the American Ballet Theatre. Her story is amazing and she is so inspiring.

———

Switch your shampoo and conditioner from time to time—don't just stick to one brand. My hair is so much happier when I swap brands every few months.

Look up! Sometimes you find an amazing building, tree, or sight that you have been walking past all this time. . . .

———

SMILE at yourself in the mirror. I used to do yoga and at the end of class the teacher would tell us to do that. I thought it was so weird and uncomfortable but then I did it and it actually made me feel happy (probably also because it meant the yoga class was finished and I could go buy a croissant . . .)

———

If you use hairbands without the metal parts, it's much better for your hair and won't make it break.

———

Read *I Capture the Castle* by Dodie Smith. SUCH a great book!

———

Drink more water—it flushes you out! I always drink two glasses as soon as I wake up.

———

Try half an avocado with lemon or reeaaaally thinly sliced tomato on toast with cream cheese.

———

Try looking at someone's face and drawing them, without lifting the pen or looking at what you are doing. You can make some masterpieces!

———

Write postcards to people—it's great to receive one.

THE

EFFEC

WAY TO

IS TO

— Amelia Earhart

50

BUT WHATEVER HAPPENS, KNOW THIS!

● ● ● ● ●

It. Will. All. Be. Okay. I mean it!

Growing up is INTENSE. Everything is unfamiliar and untested and unscripted. Everything is a first, once. You don't get to do it twice. You will get some things right the first time but, like me, with most things, you won't. You will try to avoid leaky periods, moody friends, and too much sugar. But, like many of us, you won't. Like every woman in the universe before you, eventually you will have a period crisis; your friends will be too much to handle and then the next day mean everything to you; and every now and then you are going to eat waaay too much sugar. But it's okay! Believe me, we have all done it and survived. Even when the absolute worst, most embarrassing thing happens and you feel like it's game over—it isn't! Those embarrassing moments will eventually be funny, I promise.

There have been days when I did not believe things would turn out okay, but they did anyway. The universe is huuuuge! The world is huge! And we are all just out here trying to make the most of it. Write big lists filled with BIG DREAMS, even the ones you can't imagine coming true—just write them down! So many of the things I wanted to do but was too embarrassed to even say out loud, I worked toward and eventually made happen. BELIEVE IN YOURSELF. You are your own best friend. PUSH YOURSELF—you can get there!

The one thing I always remember my dad telling me over and over when I was growing up was to leave the world a better place than I found it. At the end of the day, whatever you are doing, that should be in the back of your mind. I never, ever forget it and I check myself all the time and ask myself, "Is what I am doing useful or helpful?" It doesn't mean you have to drop everything and become an aid worker tomorrow—though kudos to you if that is your dream!—it can be simple things like helping out your friends and family, taking care of yourself so others don't need to, or being a strong and reliable friend.

Time is on your side, sister—the world is yours for the taking! Get out there and make some magic! Everything in this book is something I wish I had known when I was your age. I hope it has given you some good advice and insight for when your body switches it up on you! It's up to you—take this information and run with it, defy it, test it out, throw it to the wind, stomp on it, pin it to the wall, believe it, deny it . . . do whatever you want with it! Your body is 100 percent yours and it's AMAZING!

Go for it, little sister. See you out there somewhere on Planet Earth!

Marawa xo

from Marawa

Stella, thank you for being an endless source of happy notes and
encouraging emails—I thought editing was meant to be like a
dentist visit, but you made it like a trip to the roller rink. SINEM!
You. Legend. Nobody comes close—I knew as soon as Rachel
showed me your work you were the perfect fit for this project.
Thank you for sharing your bed with a million balloons and so
fabulously communicating the visual elements of this book.
Jo Duck—love you forever, you know that—it had to be you.

Majors, Rosa, Maz, Rachel, Clare, Obie THANK YOU for being a
part of this. YOU DA BEST. ZEZI—thank you for the emails and
reminders that this book needs to HAPPEN. FINALLY—Maman,
who was the human form of this book while I was growing up—
an endless source of medical advice, reassurance, and support.
I don't know how I managed to land the greatest mom of all time,
but I am so, so grateful I did. Thank you for always making me
feel like everything is possible. YELD FOREVER.

from Sinem

For Tijen and Nessie, who are the most inspirational and selfless women I know; Sena, who is a very strong young girl and beautiful both inside and out; Sema, who always wears a smile and is like a ray of sunshine; Lucia and Willow, for when they turn 10!; Jemma, who is working out how she can replace her pubic hair with paper ones; Lora, who is always sticking up for girls; Madeline, who got me through an all-girls school with her wit; Ella, who might find sections of this book funny; Rachel, our publisher and Stella, our skillful editor—without both their amazingness, dedication, and grit there would be no *Girl Guide*!; Chris, who lovingly assisted with making some of the paper props; and Jo, who brought my concepts and rough drawings to life with the photographs starring Marawa. And of course, MARAWA, who is such a star, sooo energizing, and an absolute joy to work with!

The Girl Guide: 50 Ways to Learn to Love Your Changing Body
Text copyright © 2017 by Marawa Ibrahim
Illustrations copyright © 2017 by Sinem Erkas
All rights reserved. Manufactured in China.
No part of this book may be used or reproduced in any manner
whatsoever without written permission except in the case of
brief quotations embodied in critical articles and reviews. For
information address HarperCollins Children's Books, a division
of HarperCollins Publishers, 195 Broadway, New York, NY 10007.
www.harpercollinschildrens.com

ISBN 978-0-06-283943-5

Art direction, graphic design, illustrations, prop making, and set
designs by Sinem Erkas
All photography starring Marawa/the Majorettes by Jo Duck
Stretch mark photos © Getty Images, Shutterstock, and Alamy
Makeup on page 115 by Natalie Young

Additional art direction for US edition by Alison Klapthor on
pages 150–151 and cover
18 19 20 21 22 SCP 10 9 8 7 6 5 4 3 2 1
❖
Originally published in the UK in 2017 by Frances Lincoln
Children's Books
First US edition, 2018

MIX
Paper from
responsible sources
FSC® C101537

IN THE MAKING OF THIS BOOK

It took 5 attempts to make the Jell-O on p.142

It took Marawa 2.26 minutes to solve the maze on p.120

Marawa and Sinem were introduced over breakfast in London

Marawa had real zits on her face being covered up by 72 googly eyes (including one that Sinem put halfway in her nose—yuck!) (p.22)

Dress rehearsals were done in Marawa's bathroom and at the Hoopermarket

All of the paper bras were made life-size

Sinem and Marawa discussed the book layout, including the vagina chapters, in various London restaurants

Marawa broke a full-length mirror at the Russian Club in London, where we did the photo shoots

Marawa shaved off ALL HER HAIR halfway through the project and we decided to re-shoot the introduction as a recreation of her ten-year-old photo

Sinem (while working out how to achieve the meditation shot) fell over and bruised her arm after trying to levitate! Luckily, Marawa is actually circus trained! (p.174)

Sinem gave Marawa homework to practice the letter poses every day for two weeks, which became Marawa's morning yoga routine

To create the paper props and sets, Sinem used approx. 30 yards of paper, 2 rolls of duct tape, 2 rolls of masking tape, 2 rolls of double-sided tape, 3 packs of sticky pads, glue, 4 yards of card stock, and 240 cups of coffee

Purple tinsel made the hair (p.65)

Marawa made 156 letters and 30 numbers with her body in one day

Sinem left her giant eyeballs (which took 5 hours to make) in a box with Marawa, which BLEW OPEN as Marawa's taxi arrived. She had to chase them all the way down the street! She kept this a secret until after the shoot (p.11)

but they were not comfy to wear

Sinem had to give up her bed for a night to create the image on p.35, as the balloons look over her whole bedroom

White PVC was used to make the yogurt on p.199

Email meetings were held everywhere as Marawa traveled between the UK, US (including Hawaii), France, Mexico, Australia, Spain, and Cuba

Sponges & dish soap were used to create the pancakes and syrup on p.207

In real life, the paper vagina illustrations are the size of a sheet of paper. Paper pubic hairs were everywhere for days after photographing them (p.52)

While arranging the paper zits, Sinem sneezed and they blew into position a lot better than how she originally had them (p.22)

MARAWA BROKE 4 WORLD RECORDS!!

Eight-time world record holder **Marawa Ibrahim** was once told she didn't have what it takes to be a performer. Today, she holds world records for the most hoops spun by an individual and the fastest 100 meters in high-heeled skates. Marawa works with hundreds of young women around the world through her award-winning hula-hoop troupe, the Majorettes.

Find Marawa online at

www.marawatheamazing.com.

Sinem Erkas is a multidisciplinary graphic artist and art director with an imaginative and stylish approach to creating images. Her practice ranges from digital artwork to photo illustrations to set design, and now human typefaces. Inspired by pop art, minimalism, and optical illusions, Sinem likes to create playful and bold artwork that makes you look twice. Based in South London, she has worked in-house as a book designer for various publishing houses. Her work has been included in London exhibitions and the Venice Biennale. Her graduate work won the "best in show" D&AD New Blood Award, and she has since acquired numerous ABCD Awards for design and illustrations.

Find Sinem online at
www.sinemerkas.com.

Simsbury Public Library
Children's Room